Simple Musings

Alisa Hope Wagner

Simple Musings
Copyright © 2017 by Alisa Hope Wagner
All rights reserved.
Marked Writers Publishing
www.alisahopewagner.com

Scriptures taken from multiple translations of the Bible.

Author photo by Lori Stead of www.wetsilver.com
Cover design By Alisa Hope Wagner

ISBN-13: 978-0692046531
ISBN-10: 0692046534

Simple Musings

Alisa Hope Wagner

Dedication

Daniel, my high school sweetheart and soul mate.

Isaac, my first-born son and prophet.

Levi, my brown-eyed boy and shepherd.

Karis Ruth, my cherished girl and graceful companion.

Christina, my amazing twin.

Thank you to Daniel Wagner and Faith Newton for taking time to proof these devotionals.

Simple Musings

"The law of the LORD is perfect (flawless), restoring and refreshing the soul; The statutes of the LORD are reliable and trustworthy, making wise the simple" (Psalm 19.7 AMP).

God makes the fool wise. This truth can be no more apparent than in my life. Growing up I was insecure, simple and foolish. Few people expected anything great from me. I was destined to be mediocre at best, and at worst I would have fallen through the cracks of mainstream America. I didn't have high expectations for myself. My only thought was to make my way through this loud, chaotic world unscathed.

But that is until God got a hold of me when I was a freshman in high school, and I enrolled in God's school for the simple. Slowly, God filled me with His wisdom as I struggled to follow His Will and Way. At forty-one, I am embarrassed when I read my diary from when I was fourteen. The proof of my life's transformation within those years is glaringly obvious. I am a fool made wise by the grace of God through His Son, Jesus Christ.

God is trustworthy. He is reliable. And He makes wise the simple. This book is a testament of that truth. The change is slow, spreading across the years. A single meditation may not show it, but an entire book reveals the conversion. I may not have arrived to my best self yet, but I'm definitely not the fool I once was.

I pray that each meditation reveals a life given over to the care of the Creator. Give your life to God, and He will make the foolish heart, the foolish mind and the foolish soul wise.

"But God chose the foolish things of the world to shame the wise; God chose the weak things of the world to shame the strong" (1 Corinthians 1.27 NIV).

Life Without Fear

"That it will never come again is what makes life so sweet." - Emily Dickinson

The truth that we have but one life creates in us a desire to live that life well. Many people believe that those of us who don't do our best in this fleeting life just don't care. But the culprit of living below God's best standard is because of two interlinking and deadly culprits.

Jesus told a parable of The Talents from Matthew 25.14-30. This story is about three men who were given talents (a bag of gold) to invest. They thought they were investing this money for their boss, but what they didn't know is that they would be personally rewarded for their investments.

The boss gave the first man 5 talents, the second man 2 talents and the third man 1 talent—each according to his ability.

The 5-talent man doubled his investments, giving his boss 10 talents in return. The boss rewarded this man by making him ruler over much.

The 2-talent man also doubled his investments, giving his boss 4 talents in return. The boss rewarded this man by making him ruler over much.

The 1-talent man had an unhealthy view of his boss, which caused him to have fear in his investments. Instead of investing his talent, he buried it, giving his boss the exact amount that had been entrusted him in the first place. The boss did not reward this man. In fact, the talent that was entrusted to him was taken away and given to someone else. The 1-talent man's unhealthy view of his boss and his fear in his investments caused him to be lazy with his talent.

If we find ourselves at a place where we feel lazy or indifferent in an area of our lives, we can blame two, interlinking culprits: We have an unhealthy view of God in our area of investments. And because of this view, we have created fear that has caused us to give up and bury our "talents."

The only solution then remains is that we must lean into God and invest in our relationship with Him. For some reason, our viewpoint in a certain area has been damaged. We must pray, read God's Word and absorb other Christian materials that help clean up our unhealthy view. Only then will the fear we carry be replaced with faith, and we can finally invest the talents that God is waiting on us to multiply!

"His lord said to him, 'Well done, good and faithful servant; you have been faithful over a few things, I will make you ruler over many things. Enter into the joy of your lord'" (Matthew 25.23 NKJV).

Cover Art Miracle

"'For my thoughts are not your thoughts, neither are your ways my ways,' declares the Lord" (Isaiah 55.8 NIV).

My husband bought my 10-year old son a used video game from Game Stop. Most of the time, the used games are just sold as a cartridge, but my son wanted the cartridge case and the cover art for the game. The store clerk was able to give him a blank cartridge case; however, the cover art for the game was not available. My son was disappointed, so the clerk told him that he could check back at a later time to see if the cover art became available.

My husband took him to another Game Stop closer to our house to see if they had the cover art, but they didn't. Then I happened to be at a book store with my kids that had a Game Stop nearby, so my son jumped out to see if they had the cover art. Sadly, he came out empty-handed again. My son was upset, and I wanted to tell him that it would be impossible to get the cover art. Most people throw them away, and the store attendants probably don't keep track of them.

But instead of telling my son to be "practical," I closed my eyes and prayed in Jesus' name in front of my three kids.

"God, You know my son's heart. You know he wants the cover art to go with his game. So I pray in Jesus' name that a store will obtain the cover art for the game and save it for my son. Amen."

All my kids said amen. It was a simple prayer, spoken quickly in my SUV before I drove back home. But I had determined myself to have faith instead of doubt. Something I was learning in my own life.

A few days later at the mall, my husband and son entered yet another Game Stop, and lo and behold, the cover art for his game was there. Not only that, the store clerk gave him the sleeve that went inside the cartridge case. In a simple yet profound way to my son, He knew that God was listening and that Jesus cared about his desires.

So many times, we think in a "practical" spirit according to the world's ways. But God's ways are higher, and He is fully capable of doing miracles—great and small ones—in our lives. God cares about us, and He wants to bless us. We simply need to determine ourselves to have faith, not doubt.

"What we have received is not the spirit of the world, but the Spirit who is from God, so that we may understand what God has freely given us" (1 Corinthians 2.12 NIV).

Copy or Obedience

"...the God who gives life to the dead and calls into being things that were not (Romans 4.17 NIV).

I read a statistic once that Christians become like the person who first introduces them to Jesus. We inherit a copy of how we were first exposed to faith. The only problem with this is that Jesus wants to express Himself in us uniquely based on the design He envisioned for us personally.

God doesn't want a copy. He wants obedience.

To break free from a certain mold that may limit the plans that God has for our lives, God will put us into situations that seem unusual or out of sync with our comfortable Christian culture. If we want to stay in obedience during these times, we will have to pour our faith into our new, unfamiliar circumstance.

Gaining new ground takes a new calling.

Of course, there are biblical truths that God will never compromise, but so much of what we see as faith is actually tradition. So much of our relationship with God is done in human-centered security and not God-centered obedience.

God moves in us to stretch and grow us.

To get us out of our mediocre religious ease, God will push us out of cookie-cutter molds. He will prune behaviors, thoughts and actions, forcing us to imagine beyond what we are used to. He will make the impossible, possible. He will call what does not exist into existence.

A closed-door calls for an open mind.

When we finally do something new, it may become tempting to repeat what worked today, thereby making copies for tomorrow. But Jesus is always moving, reaching those who are lost and taking new ground for His Kingdom. He is limitless, and He's continuously pouring our new wine of His revelation. We simply need to be empty vessels every day to catch what He's doing now.

"Jesus said, 'What is impossible with man is possible with God'" (Luke 18.27 NIV).

Stick with It

"Trust in the Lord with all your heart, and do not lean on your own understanding. In all your ways acknowledge him, and he will make straight your paths" (Proverbs 3.5-6 ESV).

I grew up on the original Nintendo Entertaining System (NES). I played Super Mario Brothers all of the sixth, seventh and eighth grade in the late 1980s. I lost interest in gaming in high school, but the hundreds of hours I clocked letting 2D games entertain my summers had trained my mind to a linear playing field.

My husband and I married in 1999 and in the first year of our marriage, we decided to purchase a new gaming system. We bought the Nintendo 64, and I tried my hand at playing Mario Kart.

For some reason, I couldn't get into the game. The graphics were amazing, but I thought that I had lost my knack at playing video games. I quickly gave up, assuming that I had just grown out of it.

Although growing out of video games was mostly true, another aspect that caused my lack of interest in the latest gaming system was that the layout was now 3D. The games weren't linear anymore, and my brain couldn't grasp the new, nonlinear perspective. I just didn't get it.

This reminds me of something similar that happens during our walk of faith. Many times, God calls us to new situations. We step out in obedience, excited about what God's going to do. But just as quickly as we step in, we instantly step back out. We lose interest and wonder if we really heard from God. We question whether He had called us or did we just imagine it.

We can't fathom what God is doing, so we instantly give up. In our limited understanding, the nonlinear playing field that God is establishing in our lives makes no sense because we are not used to it. But God is not limited to space, matter or time; and even though we may have difficulty grasping His perspective and movements at first, we shouldn't give up. Eventually, we will get it.

We must continue on the course that our first step of obedience has brought us to, trusting that He who started a good work in us will finish it to completion. If we clock enough hours into trusting God in the new situation, we will eventually get a glimpse of what God is doing. And we will realize that He is accomplishing something so much bigger than we could ever imagine. We just have to stick with it even if we don't get it at first.

"Being confident of this very thing, that He who has begun a good work in you will complete it until the day of Jesus Christ" (Philippians 1.6 NIV).

Where is Mom?

"After this I saw four angels standing at the four corners of the earth..." (Revelation 7.1 NIV).

This photo was a Timehop from two years ago on my Facebook feed today. This is me at my computer getting a sweet kiss from my middle child—my brown-eyed boy! I love this photo because it shows so much about my life.

I don't know what I was writing. I could have been working on one of my books or just writing a blog entry, but Mom writing has been a part of my kids' lives since they can remember. Seeing me at my computer with notes to the left of me and a soft blanket across my lap is normal to them.

There are four general places that my kids will find me in our home. If they are looking for me, they know to look in the kitchen, in the office, in the garage or in my closet.

The kitchen is where I serve my family. I cook and clean for them, ensuring that they eat healthy meals, yet enjoy special treats now and then.

The office is where I do my work. I write nonfiction and fiction books about Jesus, and I explore His influence and love in the lives of His people.

The garage is where exercise. I work out because it makes me feel good, and I know my body needs it.

The closet is where I pray and read my Bible. I spend time with God, and He fills me with everything I need and more.

So when my kids wonder, "Where is Mom?" They will look in these four places—where I serve, where I work, where I exercise and where I pray.

These four places may seem small and insignificant to the world, but they are the platform where God has placed me. They are my four corners (1 Chronicles 9.24).

I think if we could all find our four corners, we will see ourselves being established in the center of God's best plan for our lives. We won't be too busy or too idle. We will have the grace to achieve daily what God has called us to do without being overwhelmed or bored.

So many times, we overextend ourselves. We do too many things and make too many commitments. Everything sounds good, but not everything is possible all at the same time. Yes, seasons change. My family may see me in four different rooms years down the road, but I will be prayerful of the four places God wants me to be. I always want Jesus in the center.

Just like the Cross has four sides with Jesus hanging in the middle—I want my life to have four corners, knowing that Jesus is in the middle pouring out His love, grace, forgiveness and redemption on all that I do for Him.

"She sets about her work vigorously; her arms are strong for her tasks" (Proverbs 31.17 NIV).

Simple Musings | Alisa Hope Wagner

Shoulder Pain

"Even to your old age and gray hairs I am he, I am he who will sustain you. I have made you and I will carry you; I will sustain you and I will rescue you" (Isaiah 46.4 NIV).

I hurt my right shoulder about nine months ago. Actually, I injured my pectoral muscle, connecting right under my armpit area, which affected my shoulder movement and strength, causing pain when I worked out. So for nine months I haven't been able to lift as heavy with my right shoulder because of my injury. Whenever I do a shoulder work out, like a dumbbell shoulder press, I use weights about five or even ten pounds lighter.

But the thing about shoulders is that they are used in almost every other body workout as secondary muscles. For example, when I work my chest, doing bench press, I use my shoulders. When I work my back, doing pull-ups, I use my shoulders. When I do deadlifts, working my low back and hamstrings, I use my shoulders. Finally, when I do most bicep and triceps exercises, my shoulders are usually engaged.

Because of the pain in my right shoulder, my left shoulder began to compensate when I would do an exercise that activated both shoulders, like the bench press and pull-ups. An interesting thing began to happen. My left shoulder became stronger than my right. I started seeing more cuts and muscle striation in my left shoulder. However, just recently my left shoulder has begun to feel slight pain and limited range of movement too.

What happened? My left shoulder compensated so much for my right shoulder's pain due to a pectoral injury underneath the shoulder that it too began to strain. Whenever I would do exercises that activated both shoulders, my left would take up the slack for the right.

What's the answer? A game plan from a physical therapist with muscle movements so small that it almost seems laughable. I found out my true problem too. I have muscle imbalance. My back (mainly my mid and lower trapezius or traps) are too weak compared to my front (mainly pectoral muscles), which caused tightening and pulling of the pec muscles while doing compound exercises (working multiple muscles at once). As funny as it sounds, my left shoulder pain was caused by my right shoulder pain which was caused by my right pec injury which was caused by weakness in my back, mainly my traps.

What's my point? Many times, we have issues in our lives due to imbalance we don't know about. I had shoulder pain that was rooted in weakness of my back, which caused an injury in my pectoral muscle. My homework for physical therapy is to strengthen my mid and lower traps and stretch my pecs. There is nothing I do with my shoulders except continue to work them without hurting them.

Sometimes the pain we feel emotionally is not caused by the area that's hurting us at the moment. It may be a weakness in one area that has injured another and has limited something different! If we are dealing with an issue, we need to find the deep-seated source. Only addressing the signifier does nothing to alleviate the culprit. For example, a marital problem could be caused by something other than our spouse! We need to let the Holy Spirit, and any other resources God brings our way (books, counselors, pastors, prayer, etc.) to help us discover the true culprit for our symptoms.

"He heals the brokenhearted and binds up their wounds" (Psalm 147.3 NIV).

We may have focused so much on our strengths, ignoring our weaknesses, that our strengths are starting to hurt us because they are proportionally out of control. We must seek healing, balance and wholeness. The Holy Spirit can guide us into our healing, but we need to be willing to humble ourselves, admit our pain and do the seemingly little exercises that will promote total balance. Further, we may have to realize that the issue we keep praying about is rooted in another issue entirely.

"For I am the Lord your God who takes hold of your right hand and says to you, Do not fear; I will help you" (Isaiah 41.13 NIV).

Securing the Rock

"Then Simon Peter drew a sword and slashed off the right ear of Malchus, the high priest's slave. But Jesus said to Peter, 'Put your sword back into its sheath. Shall I not drink from the cup of suffering the Father has given me?'" (John 18.10-11 NLT).

Peter is notorious for rejecting Jesus three times. The religious leaders and many Roman soldiers took Jesus late at night into custody in order to condemn Him. John and Peter both followed Jesus to the High Priest's house and waited in the courtyard while the High Priests questioned Him.

"Simon Peter followed Jesus, as did another of the disciples. That other disciple was acquainted with the high priest, so he was allowed to enter the high priest's courtyard with Jesus" (John 18. 15 NLT).

John went into the courtyard of the High Priest's house and was able to get Peter in. The only problem is that Peter had only moments ago chopped off Malchus's ear. This man was the High Priest's assistant. Peter had broken the law and hurt a fellow Jew, and now he found himself in the home of where this man worked, where he may have lived and where a lot of people knew him. Peter tried to take control of what was happening to Jesus with his limited point-of-view, and he now faced dire consequences.

"But one of the household slaves of the high priest, a relative of the man whose ear Peter had cut off, asked, 'Didn't I see you out there in the olive grove with Jesus?' Again Peter denied it. And immediately a rooster crowed" (John 18.26 NLT).

I wonder if Peter's motivation to lie about not being a disciple of Jesus was based on the fact that he had sinned, trying to usurp God's plan of redemption for the world? If Peter hadn't done something illegal (chopping off a religious leader's ear), he may have been stronger in his faith for Christ at this time, like John was.

Peter broke the law, and because of that, he was intimidated and guilty, trying to avoid punishment caused by his disobedience. His guilty conscience, though Jesus healed the man, caused him to lose the confidence of his Christian witness to others.

This is a reminder to us when doing ministry that we should obey the fullness of God's plans in our lives and not try to take matters into our own hands, especially when they are illegal. God can give us a passion to do something, but that doesn't give us the right to not obey the law of the land (unless, of course, those laws have completely contradicted God's laws).

For example, God can give us a desire to start a business, but that does not give us license to steal money in order to accomplish His will. Or God can give us a desire to adopt a hurting child, but that does not give us right to bypass all the requirements of legal adoption. If God has given us the desire to do something, He will ensure that we can accomplish His will without breaking the law. We just have to believe that His promises are true, and He is faithful to accomplish what He has started.

With that being said, God at any time can break laws of man, supernaturally providing for us in ways that go beyond what anyone could think or image, but we need to rest in His movements, resisting the urge to step outside of His timing and plan (Acts 5.29). We don't want the fulfillment of our promises to be rooted in a personal act of disobedience because eventually, we will get found out.

Peter learned from his mistake. He was the first disciple to boldly proclaim the Gospel of Jesus Christ to the Jewish people after Jesus' ascension back to the right hand of the Father in Heaven. Peter lead thousands of people into salvation, birthing The Church. He finally saw the bigger picture of what Jesus was accomplishing with His death and resurrection, and his confidence in his Christian witness to others rocked the world.

"And I tell you that you are Peter, and on this rock I will build my church, and the gates of Hades will not overcome it" (Matthew 16.18 NIV

Second Time Around

I am learning that there is no such thing as failure with the Lord. God is so imaginative and all-powerful that even what we see as defeat can be merely a set up for a future victory. God does not view events through the limits of time; rather, He views the complete fulfillment of His plan in our lives as they appear in eternity. Jesus has the ultimate victory, so we are victorious in Christ—no matter our falls along the way.

"But thanks be to God! He gives us the victory through our Lord Jesus Christ" (1 Corinthians 15.57 NIV).

Esther is a prime example of this. She has two dinner parties with the king and her enemy, Haman, who is dead-set on destroying her people, the Jews. Esther invites both the king and her enemy to dine together with her. What an awesome example for us today! When we are being attacked by an enemy, we should always invite the King of the Universe to come to the table.

"'If it pleases the king,' replied Esther, 'let the king, together with Haman, come today to a banquet I have prepared for him'" (Esther 5.4 NIV).

The King is ALWAYS ready to sit with us!

"'Bring Haman at once,' the king said, 'so that we may do what Esther asks'" (Esther 5.5 NIV).

Esther organizes the first dinner party, but nothing happens. Was she scared? Did she chicken out? She didn't ask for the king's help to save her people, and that night she may have felt like a failure. Thankfully, though, she organizes a second dinner party for the following evening. Yes! Another chance. And this time she will be ready!

What Esther may have not known was that God was about to intervene! The night before the second dinner party, God wouldn't allow the king to sleep. The king asks his advisors to read over the previous weeks' chronicles, and he is reminded that Mordecai, Esther's uncle, had saved his life. The king owes Mordecai a favor! This would be just the thing Esther needs to muster up the courage to confront her enemy before the king.

At the second dinner party, Esther finally finds the strength to face her enemy. In Esther chapter 7 verses 5 and 6, Esther fights for her people!

"The king asked Esther, 'Who is he? Where is he—the man who has dared to do such a thing?'"

"And Esther points her finger and shouts, 'An adversary and enemy! This vile Haman!'"

And the rest of the story is biblical history. The king begins to fight for Esther and her people. The ultimate victory was always Esther's as long as she kept seeking the king! God sees beyond time, and He already knew the outcome. God's people are redeemed!

Many times, our steps of obedience lead to what feels like a dead-end or failure. And our own expectations break our hearts and cause bitterness in our soul. But we must never forget there is NO FAILURE in Jesus Christ. Everything is used for His purposes for those who continue to seek Him! Those very same steps that led to a dead-end can lead to a breakthrough the second time around!

"And we know that in all things God works for the good of those who love him, who have been called according to his purpose" (Romans 8.28 NIV).

Believe

"Jesus told them, 'This is the only work God wants from you: Believe in the one he has sent'" (John 6.29 NLT).

I'm reading the Book of John, and I'm surprised by how many times Jesus says the word, "Believe." I did a search at www.blueletterbible.org and counted over 50 times. I felt the Holy Spirit pressing the issue of belief deep within my soul because the entire premise of our faith is based on our belief in Jesus, His Word and His Work.

The opposite of belief is disbelief. And I quickly understood that the main agenda of Satan is to sow disbelief into our souls. First, our enemy wants us to have disbelief in Jesus. This is his primary goal—to prevent us from receiving salvation in the first place. Second, if the enemy can't sow disbelief into our salvation, he'll do it into our purpose.

If Satan can't prevent a Believer from going to heaven, he'll try to steal away their ability to bring anyone else into heaven. Satan knows that our true purpose in life will lead to souls finding a relationship with God through Jesus Christ. We will lead people directly into heaven or we will encourage others in their faith who will lead people to heaven. Either way our lives will produce eternal fruit when we are fulfilling God's purposes for us. And as we follow God's plan for our lives, we will mature into our best selves—the masterpiece God made us to be (Ephesians 2.10).

So our enemy will try to make us doubt everything God wants for us. He wants us to doubt our purpose, God's promises, our righteousness through Jesus Christ—anything to cause us to fall short of God's best plan for us. If we look closely at any temptation or struggle we are dealing with, it is usually rooted in disbelief. Fear, anxiety, distraction, depression, addiction, etc., can all be sourced to lacking belief in God.

We don't believe God is faithful. We don't' believe God can take care of us. We don't believe God's promises are true. We don't believe that we have joy in Christ independent of our circumstances. We don't believe God can heal our wounds and fill our emptiness. When we don't believe Jesus at His Word, we succumb to disbelief, which has a variety of negative outcomes that cause havoc in our lives.

We need to know God's Word to believe His Word. We need to know Jesus to rest our belief on Him. We can combat our disbelief only by filling our minds and hearts with His Word, the Bible. And we can spend time with God in prayer, allowing the Holy Spirit to speak to us, encourage us, remind us and fill us.

Protect and guard your belief because Jesus says that everything hinges on it.

"And when he comes, he will convict the world of its sin, and of God's righteousness, and of the coming judgment. The world's sin is that it refuses to believe in me" (John 16.8-9 NLT).

The Perfect Lamb

My oldest son did his Bible class during the summer for homeschool. He read four Christian books and wrote a book report about each one. We were running out of time, so the last book I had him read was the Gospel of John from the Bible. I was reading John, so I thought it would be nice to parallel read with him.

When my son finished the book, he spoke his initial thoughts aloud: "I wish there could have been any other sacrifice besides Jesus. Why couldn't God just sacrifice a criminal who was already condemned or someone else on their deathbed?"

When he spoke these words, I thought of all the various opinions in the world about how to achieve eternity with God. So many human-centered counterfeits to the only True Entrance to the presence of God in heaven.

"I am the door. If anyone enters by Me, he will be saved, and will go in and out and find pasture" (John 10.9 NKJV).

I asked, "Did you know that before Jesus came to this earth, God asked for the perfect, young lamb to be sacrificed for the sins of His people? Since God is outside of time, He would see this sacrifice as a signpost to His Son, Jesus."

"If the offering is a burnt offering from the herd, you are to offer a male without defect. You must present it at the entrance to the tent of meeting so that it will be acceptable to the LORD" (Leviticus 1.3 NIV).

My son nodded his head. He knew I was just about to preach about my favorite topic, Jesus.

"People started to sin because they wanted to sacrifice something other than the perfect lamb. Instead of sacrificing what was perfect, they began to sacrifice what was flawed. This corrupted God's symbolic reminder of what Jesus would accomplish. Through Jesus, God would sacrifice His absolute best, His One and Only Son, to pay for the sins of humankind."

"When you offer blind animals for sacrifice, is that not wrong? When you sacrifice lame or diseased animals, is that not wrong? Try offering them to your governor! Would he be pleased with you? Would he accept you?" says the LORD Almighty" (Malachi 1.8 NIV).

"But why is a perfect sacrifice important?" my son asked.

I thought of how to best explain this special truth to my son because all of the world's salvation and redemption rested in it.

"If you were to get caught doing something illegal, and they were going to throw you in jail, I would beg the judge to let me take your place. I love you so much that I would willingly give up my freedom for you."

My son smiled. "Thanks, Mom."

"But there is one problem," I added.

"What?" he asked.

"I'm already guilty of doing something illegal too, so I can't take your punishment because I already deserve to go to jail. The Bible says that we have all sinned and have fallen short of God's perfect standard. We are all flawed, so we can't sacrifice ourselves to atone for the sins of others."

"For everyone has sinned; we all fall short of God's glorious standard. Yet God, in his grace, freely makes us right in his sight. He did this through Christ Jesus when he freed us from the penalty for our sins" (Romans 3.23-24 NLT).

"God is a perfect Judge, and He upholds His laws or else there would be total chaos. A good judge does not compromise the truth. But God is also the perfect Father, and He loves His people and knew we would mess up. But His role as Father can't usurp His role as Judge. They are both equally important. He needed to uphold His law and His love, so He did what only a loving Father and Judge would do: He put on flesh, entered this earth, upheld the law and exchanged His perfection for our sin. Jesus became the Perfect Sacrificial Lamb for all of us. He took our guilt and gave us His innocence."

"So Jesus went to jail, so we could be free?" my son asked, grasping to understand the metaphor. "And only someone innocent can take the guilt of someone else?"

"Yes, that is why we need Jesus. He is the only One who lived a perfect life. He is the only One who can truly give His life, so we can be free. He accepted our sin and gave us His righteousness, so we could have a relationship with God. The proof that His Sacrifice on the Cross worked is that we can now have the Holy Spirit, God with us. And now that we have a relationship with God in this life, that relationship will continue after we die, and we will be in God's presence forever. We will be in heaven."

"I think I understand now. Jesus had to die for us. There couldn't be any other sacrifice," my son whispered.

"That is why Jesus in the Gospel of John, said this special truth. He is the only Way to God because no other human-centered sacrifice will ever be free of guilt except the perfect Son of God."

"Jesus answered, 'I am the way and the truth and the life. No one comes to the Father except through me'" (John 14.6 NIV).

Watching the Weather Channel, I had to make a decision. It was a Thursday late morning and I was just about to work out, but a tropical storm was becoming Hurricane Harvey and it was heading our way to Corpus Christi, Texas. Whether it would wobble south or north, I would not know until it made landfall. However, evacuation in my city was recommended at this point, not mandatory.

My kids were enjoying their last few days before school started, and I had to choose a direction. I was faced with two different, yet uniquely difficult paths. 1) I would have to prepare my kids for evacuation, hurricane-proof my house, find a hotel that allowed pets, grab everything dear to me, pack my car and get on the road away from the coast. Or 2) I would stay in my house, hurricane-proof everything, live without water and electricity for days and hunker down through the worst of the storm.

Neither decision sounded good, but I had to act quickly.

I decided to beat the traffic and get on the road. My husband who was at work stayed behind a little longer to close down shop, board up our house and then fight through endless traffic to evacuate. Less than two days later, we watched in despair as Hurricane Harvey ripped through Rockport, Texas, a town only thirty miles from our home.

The choice to evacuate our city (Corpus Christi) was voluntary, but it was mandatory for Rockport and Port Aransas and other coastal towns just north of us. Some of my family and friends stayed behind to weather the storm, while many others like me left. There were positives and negatives with both scenarios, but questioning the decision to leave or stay after the fact does no earthly good.

Sometimes in life, we have decisions to make that do not have a mandatory one-way direction. We have to choose between a rock and a hard place. The people who decided to stay to suffer without electricity and endure the scary winds and rains were no better or worse off than the people who left to suffer through hours of traffic and endure living out of suitcases. The end result was the same—we all eventually found ourselves in our homes, assessing and repairing the damage.

Yes, God many times gives us mandatory choices in life that have consequences if we disobey, but much of life's directions have several paths that lead to the same spot, yet each path is riddled with its own advantages and disadvantages. To question and compare our choices and the choices of others makes a hard decision even worse. If God is not giving us a mandate, it best just to pick a road and stick with it. There is no reason to add guilt or shame or what-ifs to an already stressful and exhausting situation.

We can make our best choice, pray to God for protection and give Him our full effort, trusting that He will guide us and keep us at peace no matter our circumstance.

"You will keep in perfect peace those whose minds are steadfast, because they trust in you" (Isaiah 26.3 NIV).

Witness of God

"The Father who sent Me has Himself testified about Me" (John 5.37 HCSB).

Jesus sat where He shouldn't and talked with a woman He shouldn't according to the Jewish tradition of the time. He wandered into Samaria where the racially mixed Jewish people lived and chatted with a woman who didn't have the best track record with men.

There is an interesting transition in how this Samaritan woman perceived Jesus.

First, she accused Jesus of being no one special: "You aren't greater than our father Jacob, are You?"

Second, she wondered if Jesus may be a little special: "I see that You are a prophet."

Third, she hinted to the prospect that Jesus was the Messiah: "I know that Messiah is coming. When He comes, He will explain everything to us."

Finally, Jesus was able to give this woman His true identity because she was open to the possibility that He may be the Savior: "I am He. The One speaking to you."

Verses gathered from the Book of John Chapter 4.

When you read the Bible, you will find that many people had these three opinions of Jesus: 1) no one special, 2) someone special or 3) the Messiah. But regardless of what people thought, Jesus knew who He was because His Heavenly Father had declared it.

Many times, God gives us promises, but we won't fully embrace them until the people around us see those promises and proclaim them over us. This, however, does not take faith and will not please God (Hebrews 11.6). We must walk in the anointing that God gives us regardless of what people think. Our beliefs, thoughts, decisions and actions should always be filtered through the witness of God, not the witness of others.

If we truly believed God's promises for our lives, we would live in those promises by faith—behaving according to what God has declared over us even when they haven't come to fruition yet. It's not "fake it until you make it." Rather, it's "faith it until you make it." So many times, we are waiting for someone to proclaim our destiny when God already has.

God's promises are always true, and we must value what He says more than what others say. Jesus said that even the witness of John the Baptist who is one of the greatest men of faith that ever lived is nothing compared to the witness of God (John 5.36). So don't wait for great men and women to declare what God has already established.

Live your promises by faith, knowing that God Himself will testify on your behalf according to His time and plan. People will have various opinions of you, but stand true to what God has declared and stay humble to His will. If the people around you walk in truth, they'll eventually see what God sees.

"Humble yourselves, therefore, under God's mighty hand, that he may lift you up in due time" (1 Peter 5.6 NIV).

Coffee Decanter

Recently, my family and I went to the Frio River for vacation. We stayed in a cabin and enjoyed five days of central Texas fun. The cabin we were staying at had everything I needed to cook our meals. The only twist was that the kitchen equipment was slightly different than what I was used to.

One thing in particular that was dissimilar was the old-fashion coffee pot. I've grown accustomed to my cappuccino maker and my Keurig, so using this retro coffee maker took some adjusting. I would fill the decanter with water and pour the water into the tank at the back of the coffee machine.

The first three days I poured the water, I made huge messes. I lost almost half my water from the pot onto the counter. This was weird to me because I always do a great job pouring liquid from one container to the next. I make sure to lift the back of the container and angle my wrist just right to ensure that no water dribbles down the throat of the container. But for some reason, I couldn't get the knack of this decanter. The more I tried, the more I spilled.

Finally, on the fourth day we were there, I decided to do something different. Instead of working so hard, I just poured the water out of the decanter into the water tank. I didn't try to lift the bottom or angle my wrist. I simply tilted the water out. And guess what? The water came straight out of the decanter and into the water tank. No spill!

The makers of the coffee pot had constructed the water to effectively pour out of the decanter with minimal manipulation and effort by the handler.

Sometimes in this life of faith, I think we try too hard to manipulate the circumstance. We know what God has called us to do, and instead of resting in Him, we struggle, strive and stress over trying to accomplish His will in our own strength. But Jesus says that His yoke is light and easy to bear (Matthew 11.30). I think much of our worry in life occurs because we are not relying on God and His design, timing and plan.

We try too hard to control the situation in our limited understanding, making a mess of things instead of simply trusting the process. I think that's why the Bible says to not lean on our own understanding and that we need to walk by faith not by sight (Proverbs 3.5 and 2 Corinthians 5.7). From now on, when I feel like I'm making a mess or I'm under too much stress, I will examine my thoughts and actions and make sure that I'm resting in God and not striving in my own effort.

"And we know that in all things God works for the good of those who love him, who have been called according to his purpose" (Romans 8.28 NIV).

New Phone Line

Recently, we bought our first-born son a new phone for his birthday, so we gave his old phone to his younger brother. My husband took our middle child to the store to get a new phone line for his phone. He was so excited to have his very own number.

The only problem was that the person who owned the phone line previously apparently had run up a lot of debt. The phone was getting calls by several collectors daily wanting information about the previous owner.

I had to take each call for about two weeks and explain to every person that the phone line had been purchased by a new owner. The debt from the old owner no longer applied to my son's number because the phone line had been bought with a price.

"For you have been bought with a price: therefore glorify God in your body" (1 Corinthians 6.20).

So many times, we drag around the debt of our old selves even though our sins have been completely paid for. Our old sinful self is dead, and we are now a new creation in Christ. Jesus died to pay for our sins from the past and every sin we commit each day. Yes, we are to learn from our mistakes, but we are not called to carry the weight of what's been wiped clean. We make the mistake by allowing the old debt to apply to our new life.

"Therefore, if anyone is in Christ, the new creation has come: The old has gone, the new is here!" (2 Corinthians 5.17).

Jesus going to the Cross to pay for our sins in no little thing. In fact, the Finished Work of Jesus Christ came at a high price, and we should not reject the freedom we have in Christ. We have the full right to declare ourselves righteous, holy and sanctified in Christ. Yes, sometimes we will act like our old selves, but this doesn't mean we have to stay in bondage to it.

"And by that will, we have been made holy through the sacrifice of the body of Jesus Christ once for all" (Hebrews 10.10).

If we simply renewed our minds every day, remembering that we are a new creation and the old self is gone, we would be less prone to behave in our old patterns. Instead, we should embrace our new selves and step out in the authority that we have through Christ. So if the enemy calls you again and reminds you of an old debt, just tell him that Jesus has paid the debt in full.

"Instead, let the Spirit renew your thoughts and attitudes. Put on your new nature, created to be like God—truly righteous and holy" (Ephesians 4.23-24).

Humiliated Adversaries

Jesus healed a woman whose body and been bent over and twisted for 18 years. He was teaching at one of the synagogues, and he stopped and called out to her.

He said, "Woman, you are free of your disability" (Luke 13.12 HCSB).

She instantly became healed.

The religious leaders were not happy because Jesus had healed on the Sabbath, and they considered healing to be work. It didn't matter that Jesus was teaching on Sabbath, which is also work. They were simply upset that Jesus could perform miracles, and they could not. They looked for any excuse to condemn Him.

What was happening at this moment was a collision of two forces: God's glory and the human counterfeit of glory. The religious leaders were being exposed as false, and they did not want to let go of their power built on pride.

Jesus called them hypocrites and exposed their double standard. They were humiliated because their self-righteousness was on display.

"When He had said these things, all His adversaries were humiliated, but the crowd was rejoicing over all the glorious things He was doing" (Luke 13.17 HCSB).

I have found that when God wants to pour out His glory onto my life, hidden areas of pride and self-righteousness in my character are displayed. God is not condemning me, but in His great love for me, He is trying to free me from the crippling effects of hidden sin. Many times, I struggle with allowing Him to expose those areas; but unless I see them, I cannot repent of them.

When I get angry and justifications rear up in my words, I must take a step back and analyze the situation. God may be trying to fill me with a greater portion of His glory, which can take the place of my pride if I confess and let go.

I may be humiliated for the moment, but the reward of gaining a more intimate relationship with God is worth it. None of us is perfect, and we will all walk through this process of going from glory to glory (2 Corinthians 3.18), learning how to die to self and resurrect in Christ (Romans 6.11). Little by little God wants to work that seed of salvation into every filament of our heart, soul, strength and mind (Philippians 2.12 and Luke 10.27).

The more our pride is exposed, the greater His glory can fill us.

Like bodybuilding, God breaks us down, so He can build us back up. With every small death to our pride, God's producing greater amounts of His glory. No one who is truly strong in the Lord has avoided this process. God's discipline in our lives proves His love for us. If He didn't care, He would just leave us bent over and twisted by sin. Instead of feeling like God's adversary when He corrects us, we should feel like His loved child.

"For the LORD disciplines those he loves, and he punishes each one he accepts as his child" (Hebrews 12.6 NLT).

Bad Mornings

"Though a thousand fall at your side, though ten thousand are dying around you, these evils will not touch you" (Psalm 91.7 NLT).

Mornings have been hard for me. It seems that the enemy loves to harass me right as I'm waking up. The devil is trying to rob me of my first waking moments, so he can spoil my entire day. After several weeks of being victim to his ploys, I finally learned to aggressively meditate on Scripture right when my eyes open.

I know that the enemy is just waiting to bombard my mind with doubts, fears and insecurities. He sees my faithfulness, and he wants nothing more than to shake my belief. If he can entangle my thoughts, my emotions and actions will fall prey.

It feels like the enemy has revved up his game, so I have leaned into God and His Word. I instantly listen to Christian podcasts, play anointed music or grab my Bible and begin to read. The Spirit-filled words I listen to and read act like a balm covering my mind and heart. The enemy's words lose their power as God's Spirit embraces me with protection and authority.

It makes sense why King David sought God every morning. His enemies were always creeping around him, and he needed to refresh in God's Word and Spirit to start his day in strength and peace.

"O Lord, hear me as I pray; pay attention to my groaning. Listen to my cry for help, my King and my God, for I pray to no one but you. Listen to my voice in the morning, Lord. Each morning I bring my requests to you and wait expectantly" (Psalm 5.1-3 NLT).

To me, it's not about having enough time each morning to commune with God and read His Word. I have to spend time with Him. I have to read my Bible. I enjoy being with God because He is my "fortress and my deliverer" (Psalm 18.2). I need His peace and joy throughout my day; otherwise, I'll be vulnerable and unable to protect myself against the enemy's attacks.

Because I desire to live for God by seeking His will and sharing my faith, the enemy doesn't like it. In fact, he hates it. The devil may not know exactly what I'm writing each day, but he sees God's light shining from my words. And the Bible says that the devil is incessantly accusing me with anything he can get his hands on. To be sure, the more I write for God, the more the enemy attacks me.

Our enemy knows the end of the story, and he will be defeated by two things: the Blood of the Lamb and the words of our testimony. When we begin to walk in the authority of Jesus Christ and start sharing our faith story with others, we will have a powerful hand in defeating the devil. As we begin to take ground for God's Kingdom, the enemy will fight back, pulling out all the stops to bring us down.

We must not let him. We are not doing anything wrong when we find ourselves under spiritual attack. On the contrary, we are doing something right! That is why the enemy is trying to attack our minds first thing in the morning, so he can neutralize the threat early. Instead of falling victim to his accusations, we can go to God's Word and listen to what the Holy Spirit wants to share with us. When we find our power in Christ, the enemy's tactics will fall by the wayside.

"It has come at last—
   salvation and power
and the Kingdom of our God,
   and the authority of his Christ.
For the accuser of our brothers and sisters
   has been thrown down to earth—
the one who accuses them
   before our God day and night.
And they have defeated him by the blood of the Lamb
   and by their testimony.
And they did not love their lives so much
   that they were afraid to die."
- (Revelation 12.10-11 NLT)

Don't Curse Blessings

"...Each one must be fully convinced in his own mind" (Romans 14.5 HCSB).

My 13-year old son talks to me every night before he goes to bed about any worries, struggles, excitements or blessings from that day. This particular evening, I could see he had a thought that troubled him. He had earned $100 for filming and making a video for my niece's wedding, and after paying his tithe, he had spent almost all of it on filming and gaming gadgets he had been wanting.

"I watched a TED talk, Mom," he began. "And the guy said that we should be saving money. He said that kids my age have no concept of money and that we just spend it all without trying to set some aside."

"Yes," I said. "It's good to save for a rainy day."

"But I only $5 left from my wedding video. Was it wrong for me to spend all my money? Now I feel bad about everything I bought."

I saw the look of doubt on his face, and instantly recognized what he was feeling. I have felt it all my life, and God had been teaching me how to break free from the cycle of cursing my own blessings.

"Wait here," I said. "God showed me something a few days ago that I want to share with you."

I ran downstairs and into my closet, and I kneeled toward my highlighted Bible on the carpeted floor. I looked at my journal next to the Bible and found the chapter in Romans that I had written down with some notes. I went upstairs determined to help free my son from such a seemingly small but potent curse-prospective.

He was waiting for me in his bed, so I stood and began to read what I had highlighted: "Do you have a conviction? Keep it to yourself before God. The man who does not condemn himself by what he approves is blessed. But whoever doubts stands condemned..." (Romans 14.22-23 HCSB).

"Were you fully convinced about those items you wanted to buy? Did they make you happy and have they blessed your life?" I asked him.

"Yes," he said, nodding his head.

"Then do not doubt it with your words or else you will ruin all your blessings that you worked hard to buy. Instead of being blessed, you will be condemned in your own heart. And then your $100 will truly be wasted. Do you understand?" I asked.

"Yes, I think I do," he said, his expression lightening.

"As long as you are not going against God's Word and as long as God didn't tell you otherwise, it is completely fine to bless yourself with the money you have earned. If you want to save money next time, that will be great. But don't curse a blessing by harboring doubt. You were fully convinced to buy those things, they made you happy, so don't ruin the blessing by doubting."

"I see what you're saying!" he said, enthusiastically. "Thank you, Mom."

I thought to myself how sad that I'm 40 and still struggling with this curse-prospective, condemning blessings with my own thoughts of doubt. Doubt is the killer of joy. I think that's why the Bible says don't look to the left or right because that hesitation will always lead to doubt, and doubt is certainly not of God (Proverbs 4.27). Doubt is the opposite of trust, and we are to trust our Heavenly Father because He truly loves and enjoys us.

If our choice does not go against the Bible and the leading of the Holy Spirit in our lives, we should enjoy the blessing without allowing doubt to sneak in and destroy our joy. If Satan can't prevent the blessing, he'll simply try to condemn it. So don't let him. Stand firm on your conviction and be blessed.

"I pray that God, the source of hope, will fill you completely with joy and peace because you trust in him.

Then you will overflow with confident hope through the power of the Holy Spirit" (Romans 15.13 NLT).

The Shrewd Manager

"So the master commended the unjust steward because he had dealt shrewdly. For the sons of this world are more shrewd in their generation than the sons of light" (Luke 16.8 NKJV).

Many of Jesus' parables are difficult to understand because God wants us to dig in and search for the gems of truth. This is especially true for The Parable of the Shrewd Manager. Jesus was speaking before the religious leaders of the time, so His words hit many marks among the people as they still do today. The gist of the story is that there was a manager of a rich man's estate, and the manager was unfaithful with his master's money, squandering it selfishly. The master found out and told the manager to make account for his money handling because he was about to lose his job.

The manager knew he would be fired soon, so he persuaded all the people around him into multiplying the mismanagement of his master's money. He made friends with others by allowing them to benefit from the exploitation of his master's estate. In effect, the manager multiplied his unrighteousness beyond his personal life and into the lives of everyone in his sphere of influence.

When the master found out, he complimented the manager on one single truth: he had "dealt shrewdly" by multiplying his efforts. He was unrighteous with a little and became unrighteous with much.

Jesus was pinpointing the religious leaders who were not only mismanaging the law for themselves, but they were entangling the Jewish people into unrighteousness, as well. The corruption in the religious systems of that day became extremely evident when Jesus went to the Temple and turned the tables because His House had become a "den of thieves" (Matthew 21.13).

The religious leaders had been so cunning, intelligent and wise in the proliferation of their white-washed false piety that almost the entire Jewish nation had succumbed.

But there was a Voice in the Wilderness breaking through the lies, deception and ignorance that was layered thickly on the backs of the people, enslaved to the pride of God's corrupt managers (Isaiah 40.3 and John 1.23). Finally, Jesus would form a new system of grace, which would be multiplied from within Himself to His disciples and onto the rest of the world.

Today we can glean several things from this The Parable of the Shrewd Manager

1) As God's managers, we need to be faithful with the grace God has given each of us in our personal lives, so we can multiply this faithfulness in the lives of those around us. "Whoever is faithful with very little is also

faithful in much, and whoever is unrighteous in very little is also unrighteous in much (Luke 16.10 HCSB).

2) As God's managers, we must be shrewd (wise, intelligent, prudent) about our faith and multiply it to the people around us, freeing them from the enslavement of sin. The only way we can truly be shrewd is if we have the Mind of Christ. We can seek Him daily and renew our minds away from the systems of this dark world and into the systems of God's Kingdom (1 Corinthians 2.16 and Romans 12.2).

3) As God's managers, we should never make friends with people by exploiting God's grace, saying what people want to hear even though it's destroying their lives. This is multiplying unrighteousness. "They dress the wound of my people as though it were not serious. 'Peace, peace,' they say, when there is no peace" (Jeremiah 8.11 NIV).

4) As God's managers, we should be about our Master's business, not our own profit, glory, influence, platform and name. This doesn't mean that God won't bless us; it simply means that we seek His Kingdom first. "But seek first his kingdom and his righteousness, and all these things will be given to you as well" (Matthew 6.33 NIV).

5) As God's managers, we must each rise up so the Church can rise up. Jesus said that "The harvest is plentiful but the workers are few" (Matthew 9.37 NIV). Unrighteousness is being multiplied faster and with greater intensity than faithfulness. Division, pride and self-promotion are damaging the Church's effectiveness. Our only hope is to

abandon ourselves to God, giving Him total authority and presence. Only then we can break through the walls of resistance for ourselves and others.

6) As God's managers, we can't just lead people to Christ and leave them there. Yes, they are saved, but we need multipliers—people who create faithfulness in the lives of those around them. People long to have a purpose, but many times they need spiritual "fathers" and "mothers" to guide them and set them in their Promise Land. Jesus modeled this when He took 12 disciples under His wing, and each one (replacing Paul for Judas the betrayer) multiplied the Kingdom of God insurmountably (Luke 6.12-16).

7) Finally, as God's managers, we must look for a fresh Word from God each day. We cannot apply yesterday's revelation to today's need. Yes, "Jesus Christ is the same yesterday and today and forever," but He is constantly moving His Kingdom purpose into fruition. We need to keep up or we will fall behind (Hebrews 13.8 NIV).

Carrying Jars

Carrying jars of water in ancient times was an important but very menial task. Water was necessary for living, but taking time to bring jars to the well and carry them home was considered a humbling task meant for the lowly. But the amazing truth is that breakthroughs are found on the other side of this seemingly ordinary work.

Rebekah was found by Abraham's servant while she was carrying water. She offered the servant a drink and watered his camels. Her life changed in an instant as she was betrothed to Isaac. She would play a significant role in God's story on earth, becoming one of the great matriarchs in the Bible. All because she carried a jug of water.

"Before he had finished praying, he saw a young woman named Rebekah coming out with her water jug on her shoulder..." (Genesis 24.15 NLT).

The Samaritan woman was carrying her jar to Jacob's Well to get water when she happened to run into Jesus, the Son of God. This woman received salvation and became the portal for an entire city to receive Living Water from the Messiah. All because she carried a jug of water.

"The woman left her water jar beside the well and ran back to the village, telling everyone, 'Come and see a man who told me everything I ever did! Could he possibly be the Messiah?' So the people came streaming from the village to see him" (John 4.28-30 NLT).

Jesus' disciples wanted to prepare the Passover meal. Jesus told two of them to go into a city and follow a man carrying a jug of water. This man would lead them to the upper room where they would share the Last Supper, and Jesus would symbolically serve His Blood and Body to His disciples. This is the example of the greatest breakthrough of all. A nameless man (a metaphor for the Holy Spirit) led them to their final destination of rest before the events of the Crucifixion. God's Spirit humbled Himself to doing a lowly task for the benefit of all humankind, and we would have the honor to partake in the Sacrifice of Jesus.

"He replied, 'As you enter the city, a man carrying a jar of water will meet you. Follow him to the house that he enters, and say to the owner of the house, "The Teacher asks: Where is the guest room, where I may eat the Passover with my disciples?" He will show you a large room upstairs, all furnished. Make preparations there'" (Luke 22.10-12 NIV).

A lot can happen when we carry jars of water on our backs. Our task may seem menial and we might see others doing more "important" things, but God sees our work and He knows our heart. He can provide a breakthrough at any moment, but it takes time to create a servant's heart out of a selfish one. God is transforming us from the inside out. Every day, God has new and fresh revelation of Himself to give us. We simply need to take time to dip into the Well of His Living Water and receive. Then we can carry this revelation with us daily and offer it to the people God brings into our lives. God will fulfill His promises that He has planned for us. We simply need to continue our work with a humble heart and carry the love, grace and salvation of Jesus wherever we go.

"But we have this treasure in jars of clay to show that this all-surpassing power is from God and not from us" (2 Corinthians 4.7 NIV).

Die Fighting

Peter was willing to die for Jesus, but in the wrong way. Before Jesus was crucified, He told His disciples that they would all leave Him. However, Peter insisted that He would die for Jesus; which, in fact, was true. But this sacrifice would have been for self-glory, not God's glory.

JESUS: "Then Jesus said to them, 'Tonight all of you will run away because of Me...'" (Matthew 26.31 HCSB).

PETER: "'Even if I have to die with You,' Peter told Him, 'I will never deny You!' And all the disciples said the same thing" (Matthew 26.35 HCSB).

JESUS: "Jesus replied, 'I tell you the truth, Peter—this very night, before the rooster crows twice, you will deny three times that you even know me'" (Mark 14.30 HCSB).

After Jesus finished praying with His disciples at the Garden of Gethsemane, a huge mob entered the scene late at night. These men had swords and clubs, and were ready for a fight. The thick tension between Jesus and the army mounted when Peter took out his sword and sliced a man's ear right off. There was no way that Jesus and His 12 disciples would have conquered this massive armed mob.

Peter was ready for battle and willing to die for Jesus, but Jesus reprimanded him.

Jesus healed that man's ear and told Peter: "Sheathe your sword! Am I not to drink the cup the Father has given Me?" (John 18.11 HCSB).

Peter willingly sacrificed, worked and took risks for Jesus according to his own terms, but when he was asked to submit to the Father's terms, he ran away and denied Jesus three times.

When we look at this story, we have to ask ourselves, "Am I sacrificing in the name of Jesus for my own epic glory or am I submitted to the Father's will, humbling myself to a path that makes no sense right now?" The process of God's glory being established in our lives takes time and takes us out of center stage. His glory is about Jesus saving the world, not our ability to fight.

Jesus Christ was about to spill His Atoning Blood over all the earth. But this glory only happened after great humility. Many times, we think we are fighting God's battles, but we are delaying a mass outpouring of His glory in our lives. We are so busy fighting for Him but not truly submitted to Him.

We unsheathe our swords in front of the multitude and yell out a victory cry, but when God asks us to take up our cross and truly trust His will and way, we run away denying that He ever spoke to us. Other times we stay so busy fighting battles in the name of God, that we have no time to listen to God and hear what He has to say. We would rather the glory of the fight than the humility of the wait.

Jesus reprimanded Peter for fighting because Peter's mindset was not eternal. This small war that Peter was waging in the name of Jesus would have usurped Jesus' death on the Cross, bypassing the redemption of the world. He thought he was fighting for Jesus, but he was actually fighting against Jesus!

Let us each look at our battles that we are fighting in the name of Jesus and ask ourselves, "Is this truly what God wants or what I want? Am I submitted to God's will or my own will? Am I so busy fighting that I don't have time to listen to God?"

If we look within ourselves and analyze our motives, we may realize that all along we've been fighting against God's hand and Jesus is no longer by our side in the fight. He's waiting for us to get so worn out fighting that we finally turn our attention back to Him and obey His will.

"But Samuel replied, 'What is more pleasing to the LORD: your burnt offerings and sacrifices or your obedience to his voice? Listen! Obedience is better than sacrifice, and submission is better than offering the fat of rams'" (1 Samuel 15.22 NLT).

Epaulette Shark

The epaulette shark walks on land….well, kind of. It is the only shark that lives in water so shallow that when the tide recedes at night, the shark is literally landlocked. It is able to live more than one hour without oxygen by slowing or shutting down many of its major bodily systems. Then it uses its club-like fins to push off the seafloor, moving along the land with ease.

While other sharks have to retreat in low tide, the epaulette shark can "walk" from tidal pool to tidal pool, eating its fill on all the prey left behind. This shark is undisturbed by other predators and the transient land becomes its feeding ground. God designed that specific shark to go where other sharks can't go.

Just like the epaulette sharks, God designed each of us to enter places other people can't go in order to reach His people with the Good News of Jesus Christ. We are all specifically wired to enter certain "tidal pools" of darkness, bringing the Light of Christ with us (Matthew 5.14). However, many times we don't realize that we have these special abilities until God recedes the waters of our comfort zones.

When we feel like fish out of water, we must not retreat back to easy currents. God will bring forth capabilities that we never knew we had, which are only triggered by this "transient" situation. We may flounder a bit at first, but God created us into a unique masterpiece perfectly suited for our new environment (Ephesians 2.10). We will soon adapt and excel.

For this reason, we should never compare ourselves to others because they are reaching different tidal pools than we are. Also, we should only discern the work of others by their fruit (Matthew 7.15-20). What they are doing may seem weird to us, but they are reaching a different people group who are out of our sphere of influence. If they are spreading the Good News of Christ, and people are being saved and transformed, we should pray for them, not criticize them.

Jesus says that the harvest is plentiful, but the workers are few. There are fields of opportunity before us. We can keep our eyes on our tidal pools, allowing God to transform us into our best design for the work He has for us. Also, we can encourage those who are making a difference in God's kingdom, trusting that there is plenty of harvest for us all.

"Then He said to His disciples, 'The harvest truly is plentiful, but the laborers are few. Therefore pray the Lord of the harvest to send out laborers into His harvest'" (Matthew 9.37-38 NKJV).

Many years ago, my family and I went to our friends' house for a July 4th celebration. The condo where the festivities were held was on the top floor of a high-rise situated right on the waterfront. The city popped fireworks every year on the shoreline, and from the vantage point of this condo, the explosions were right in front of us.

My daughter was young, only two or three at the time, and the fireworks scared her. I had to take her behind closed doors to calm her fears. She missed out on the amazing display because fear overwhelmed her.

Years later, my daughter loves fireworks. She has matured to the point that her awe of the fireworks overpowers her fear, and the exhilaration of the entire light display thrills her to no end.

Recently, I asked God why He hasn't shown Himself more powerfully in my life. He speaks to me daily, and I hear Him in whispers, promptings and life metaphors. But I read Jesus' Words in the Bible, and they are promises of more.

"Very truly I tell you, whoever believes in me will do the works I have been doing, and they will do even greater things than these, because I am going to the Father. And I will do whatever you ask in my name, so that the Father may be glorified in the Son. You may ask me for anything in my name, and I will do it" (John 14.12-14 NIV).

Jesus changed lives. Yes, He changed them as a teacher, shepherd and evangelist. But He also changed them as a prophet, healer and miracle-maker. He taught hard truths from a mountaintop, but He also walked on water through the storms (Matthew 5 and Matthew 14). People experienced an explosion of God's mercy, grace and love through Jesus Christ during the massive spiritual drought of their time.

Today people are living in a spiritual drought. They long to know that there is a God who speaks and moves on behalf of His people. They need an explosion of Jesus in their lives. I realized that I have been too scared to allow God to ignite fully in my life. I don't mind God's whispers, but I've feared His thunder. But people are waiting to hear and experience God.

"When the people saw the thunder and lightning and heard the trumpet and saw the mountain in smoke, they trembled with fear. They stayed at a distance and said to Moses, 'Speak to us yourself and we will listen. But do not have God speak to us or we will die.' Moses said to the people, 'Do not be afraid. God has come to test you, so that the fear of God will be with you to keep you from sinning.' The people remained at a distance, while Moses approached the thick darkness where God was" (Exodus 20.18-21 NIV).

I demonstrate my lack of trust when my fear overpowers my awe of God. If I truly trusted God's love for me, I would desire the fullness of His presence and glory in my life. I wouldn't shut doors to the scary, hard stuff. I would open them wide to every aspect of life with Jesus. I must walk by faith into the thick glory of His presence, and spend time with Him according to His terms, not mine. People need to experience a God who is alive, vibrant and in love with His people. I can be one of many "fireworks" ignited for Jesus and lighting up this dark world with His glory.

"Trust in the Lord with all your heart and lean not on your own understanding; in all your ways submit to him, and he will make your paths straight" (Proverbs 3.5-6 NIV).

Chasing Rainbows

When I was around 8 years old, I saw a rainbow in the field that stretched across the horizon from my backyard. I lived in Kansas at the time, and I sat on our makeshift swing set, staring at the endless, golden wheat fields.

The brilliant rainbow was large, and I knew in my heart that I could probably reach the end of it if I tried. I thought of the pot of gold waiting for me—maybe even a leprechaun wearing a green hat with a four-leaf clover poking out of it.

Although I could image making it to the end of the rainbow and what I would do with my treasure once I found it, I never left my swing. I did not have faith that there would be a pot of gold and leprechaun at the end of the rainbow. The promise was only a fairytale. My efforts would leave me disappointed and empty-handed.

The Bible says, "In the same way, faith by itself, if it is not accompanied by action, is dead" (James 2.17 NIV).

If we truly believed in God's promises, our faith would get us out of our cozy swing set and into the wheat fields before us. If we never respond to God's promises with our action, we demonstrate to Him and to the world that—

although we can imagine it all—we do not believe that God will do what He says He will do. We believe that His promise is only a fairytale.

But unlike the pot of gold and the leprechaun, God's promises are true. He is the King of the Universe, and He will bring to fruition everything He says He will accomplish.

God wants us to get up and respond to our God-given dreams because we believe they are real and He is more than capable of accomplishing His great plans for our life. Our faith will produce actions rooted in belief, and it will also create a waiting that's anchored in hope.

What we will come to realize is that the end of our rainbow is much farther away then we could ever image, and the path to reaching our breakthrough is much harder to achieve than we could ever anticipate. But it will be the journey that shapes us into the image of Christ, so that when we do reach our pot of gold, our sole focus will be to be about our Father's business (Luke 2.49).

So let us leave the safety of our swing set and take a risk in the fields of God's promises, trusting that our efforts will not come back void and we will grasp onto the abundant life that God has planned for us (Isaiah 55.11 and John 10.10).

"For no matter how many promises God has made, they are 'Yes' in Christ. And so through him the 'Amen' is spoken by us to the glory of God" (2 Corinthians 1.20 NIV).

Cutting Apples

"But he said to me, 'My grace is sufficient for you, for my power is made perfect in weakness.' Therefore I will boast all the more gladly about my weaknesses, so that Christ's power may rest on me" (2 Corinthians 12.9 NIV).

I wanted to spend some time with my 8-year old daughter, so I asked her to prepare dinner with me. We were making a sweet potato hash. Part of this recipe called for sliced apples. My daughter had helped me brown the sausage and put the sliced sweet potatoes in the pan, so now it was time for her favorite part—the sweet stuff. She loves chocolate, fruits and anything sweet!

I sliced the apples and handed her a butter knife. I asked her to cut off the apple core remnants on each slice of apple. I could tell she was having a difficult time lining the butter knife across the core. She didn't want to take too much of the apple flesh off, so precision was necessary. When she finally got the blunt blade exactly where she wanted it, she struggled with cutting. She didn't have the strength to bring the butter knife through the apple flesh.

I gently put my hand over hers and helped her with each step. After we were done, she looked so pleased. At dinner, we let everyone know that Kiki and I made the hash together. The truth is, though, that there would have been no way for her to prepare the dish on her own. She needed her mother's guidance, strength and encouragement.

Many times, God has us do things that are way beyond our ability. He doesn't do this to make us fail; He does this so His strength will be made perfect in our weakness. The end result will bless others, but His main objective is truly to spend time with us. Why? Because Jesus created us, died for us and loves us. He wants to have an ever-growing personal relationship with us. He willingly shares His glory in us, allowing us to take partial credit of fulfilling His amazing plan of earth, so we can have fellowship with Him.

"I have given them the glory that you gave me, that they may be one as we are one—I in them and you in me—so that they may be brought to complete unity. Then the world will know that you sent me and have loved them even as you have loved me" (John 17.22-23 NIV).

Open Doors

My 8-year-old son pulled on the door over and over again, frustrated that it wouldn't open. I could see one of the teachers through the vertical window, taking in the moment and biding her time. She wanted to give him a few extra seconds of hopelessly yanking on the handle before opening it and commencing her one-minute lecture.

The door challenge became a lesson in locked doors and how they will not magically open on their own. I understand her point, and I value her instruction to my son. That being said, I too have a point of my own about locked doors. I know that there is a God in heaven who has the keys to every single one!

Yes, the door was locked, and, yes, there was no way he would have opened it on his own. However, we serve a God that can open every locked door that we face! Don't we want our kids believing in the impossible? As Christian parents, shouldn't we be teaching about Christ's strength in our weaknesses (2 Corinthians 12.9)?

My son might not have been able to open that door, but there is a God who thinks highly of his child-like faith, and He could have blown that door right off its hinges!

You never know—my son could have pulled the door opened by faith if I had been prepared with the right verses to encourage him!

Every day, we subject our kids to the limitations of reality and the natural world, and then we expect them to grow up into faith-filled, miracle believing Christian adults. We tell them what they can and cannot do, forgetting one important detail found in Matthew 19.26: "…but with God all things are possible!"

We can have a new generation of relentless, door-busting, faith-wielding Christians if only we stand on the promise that there is nothing too hard for God. So the next time we see a young boy or girl yanking on a door handle, let them give it their best shot! And while they tug and pull, we can encourage them with the ultimate truth—that door may be locked, but we serve a God who has the master key!

"I know your works. Behold, I have set before you an open door, which no one is able to shut. I know that you have but little power, and yet you have kept my word and have not denied my name" (Revelation 3.8 ESV).

Nitpicking

My family just left a season of nitpicking—no, not for flaws or mistakes, but literally picking nits out of each other's hair! My middle son received lice from a friend, and from there we all fell prey. The only person unaffected was my husband, so I assume lice don't like gelled, short hair.

To say this was one of my worst nightmares is an understatement. Not only do these small parasites freak me out (I won't even look at their picture on the Internet,) they also cause so much havoc in people's lives.

We had to call family and friends. We had to wash sheets, pillowcases, pillows, blankets, dolls, coats, clothes, etc. I had a pile of laundry halfway up to the ceiling next to the laundry machines! We had to wash each person's hair and painstakingly sift through every strand with a tiny, metal nitpicking pick.

Even though all the lice were killed by the shampoo, we spent hours trying to pick the nits! And if you miss just a few, the entire mess happens again. Three times in a one-month period, we had to battle lice—three sets of phone calls, three stacks of laundry, three times of washing and picking at hair. And all of this occurred at the worst possible time! I was publishing three books, we were leaving on a family vacation and I was in the final stages of preparing for a bodybuilding competition.

However, during this month of chaos, I did something different. Instead of complaining to God, I started thanking Him for nits! My kids thought I was crazy, but I knew God had allowed this nit-infestation for some reason, and I was going to praise Him in the storm. My praise should not be circumstantial; rather, it should be based on an unchanging and mighty God!

Now that our family has been nit free for a while, I can look back and know that I did not let my praise be detoured by something as tiny as parasites. Parasites do not change the awesomeness and goodness of our God! I've come to realize that my fears will never overshadow the power of God, and I can and should praise Him during the good times and the bad!

"I will praise the Lord at all times.
I will constantly speak his praises.
I will boast only in the Lord;
let all who are helpless take heart.
Come, let us tell of the Lord's greatness;
let us exalt his name together."
- (Psalm 34.1-2 NLT)

Meditation

"I lie awake thinking of you, meditating on you through the night" (Psalm 63.6 NLT).

Meditation has become such a confusing word in our culture that its meaning and purpose seem mysterious to many of us. However, meditation simply means a continued or extended thought and reflection. We can meditate on ourselves, on a television show, on homework, on our children, on our worries, doubts and insecurities. We can meditate on anything in this world—good or bad.

The highest form of meditation we can achieve, however, is meditating on God. We can meditate on God because of Jesus' sacrifice on the Cross and the work of the Holy Spirit in our lives. Meditation on the Source of all that is holy, good, perfect and glorious will not only encourage us, it will revolutionize our lives.

Meditating on God and His Holy Word is like forming an artery from His Spirit to ours, pumping our lives full of love, joy, peace, security and hope. And our spirit will change the trajectory of our physical, mental and emotional well-being. God says that there is life and death in words, and meditation produces a supernatural language of Living Water flowing into us.

Are you stressed, worried, scared? Don't meditate on the waves of life; meditate on your Holy Father, and I promise you'll be asleep in the midst of the storm, flooded by the peace in your soul. Take time today to focus all your attention on your loving God. He has an abundance of love, healing, truth and beauty He wants to give you. He died to be able to have a relationship with you, so take that precious gift today and open it.

Grab your Bible, go to your closet, close the door and get alone with God. Whether you spend five minutes or fifty, I promise you that you will transform your day.

"The tongue has the power of life and death, and those who love it will eat its fruit" (Proverbs 18.21 NIV).

Recently, my husband and I turned in my 8-year-old SUV, so I could get a newer model. My new SUV has a backup camera that shows me not only where I'm going in reverse, but it also gives me a digital projection of my progress. For example, it tells me where my car's trajectory is heading if I continue backing up in the same direction.

At first, I did not use this video. Maybe I didn't trust it or I just wasn't used to it—but I continued to crane my neck so I could tilt my head behind me as I backed out of my long, windy driveway. After weeks of ignoring the backup video, I finally decided to test it out. I kept my eyes on the screen and backed out slowly as I followed the two indicator lines on the video.

At one moment, I was sure I was about to drive into my front lawn, but I forced myself to stare at the screen, depending on the information provided to me by my car's computer. To my surprise, I drove perfectly onto my street without hitting a mailbox or a curb. Wow! The rear camera does work. Car designers truly know what they are doing!

The same goes for God. Sometimes we strain to see where we are going in life, and we exhaust ourselves by constantly trying to project the trajectory of our actions. However, there is a much easier way. If we simply keep our eyes on God and trust the indicators of the Holy Spirit, we can be confident that we will arrive exactly where we need to be. No guesswork. No craning. Just an irrefutable trust in the power and authority of our almighty God!

Since God designed all of life, we can obey His parameters, knowing that He is faithful to His promises and true to His Word. We don't have to worry—we simply need to keep our eyes on the Lord and obey His promptings. Is God telling you to keep your eyes on Him today? Is there something in your life that is causing your neck to crane? Will you go to His Word and listen for His voice?

God will display everything you need to be victorious today. Believe that He knows what is best and rest in His faithful love and care!

"Trust in the Lord with all your heart
and lean not on your own understanding;
in all your ways submit to him,
and he will make your paths straight" (Proverbs 3.5-6 NIV).

Messy Harvest

"Without oxen a stable stays clean, but you need a strong ox for a large harvest" (Proverbs 14.4 NLT).

If we complain about the mess that comes with our calling, we are in essence begrudging the purpose that God has given us. Every purpose will have its problems. Every portion of territory God entrusts to us will have its mishaps. There's no way around it.

When we pray for God to expand our sphere of influence, we might as well also pray for more battles to overcome, more fires to put out and more needs to be met. Without problems our purpose would have no meaning.

God does not give us a platform, so we can be blessed; He gives us a platform, so we can bless others. If we are to be like Christ, we will need to be a "last-place servant."

"He sat down, called the twelve disciples over to him, and said, "Whoever wants to be first must take last place and be the servant of everyone else" (Mark 9.35 NLT).

All of us have our problems, but only the strong can overcome their own battles while helping others achieve victory too. Not flinching at our dirt-stained lives as we plow the hearts of God's people is powerful. Just like the oxen never veer while they sludge through the muddy fields, we can stay yoked to Christ, knowing that our soiled feet are tracking prints for God's glory throughout the earth.

The harvest we offer to God may never be tidy, perfect and clean; but it can be an abundant crop, overflowing to the lives of others.

"But among you it will be different. Whoever wants to be a leader among you must be your servant..." (Matthew 20.26 NLT).

Do Something Bad

My three kids went to a Vacation Bible School (VBS) at a local church. Though this church is not the one that my family attends, it is still a Bible-believing church and definitely part of the Body of Christ. This particular church has a skate park for skateboarding enthusiasts. During VBS, my 8-year son watched as the older boys skated over the ramps and down the poles with their skateboards.

My son has his own board and helmet, and we take him to the park every once in a while. But when he saw those boys doing their stunts at the skate park, he would talk about nothing else. He begged me every day to take him to the skate park so he could practice his moves. The church is on the other side of town, so I could never find the time to just swing by and let him skate. Finally, one day I was determined to get him to the skate park. I packed the kids' lunches, and we made the trip over to the church. My son could not wait to skate, and I wanted to motivate him as much as possible.

When we got there, my son put on his helmet, grabbed his skateboard and walked quickly into the park. I sat down ready to cheer him on and take photos. My son is still a beginner, so he struggled with simply staying on the board. His hopes of skirting the ramp's edge and sliding down the pole with his board floundered. He could barely make it one foot up the ramp before jumping off of his board.

I yelled encouragements, and after 10 minutes, my son was done. It was obvious he was disappointed, but I congratulated him on an amazing first skate at the park.

"I wasn't as good as the other boys," he said looking down.

"You are still learning," I encouraged. "If you keep practicing, one day you will be just as good as the other boys."

He looked up at me with his thoughtful brown eyes.

"Don't forget," I continued. "You have to be bad at something before you can become good at it. I'm proud that you began the journey to becoming the best skateboarder ever!"

He smiled and said, "I can't wait to come back again!"

And that's a truth that resonates: We have to be bad at something before we can become good at it.

Many of us never try new things because we are not willing to be bad at something. But if God is calling us to something new, we have to be willing to humble ourselves and make mistakes, learn from others and take a chance.

Each time we let ourselves be bad at it, we get one step closer to mastering it. Every person who excels in a certain area was once terrible. Even raw talent needs to be cultivated. So let us get over ourselves and try something new!

"See, I am doing a new thing! Now it springs up; do you not perceive it? I am making a way in the wilderness and streams in the wasteland" (Isaiah 43.19 NIV).

Hammering Fork

As we were eating breakfast this morning, my husband told our oldest son—who may have been talking more than he was eating—to put his fork to work. My son instantly smiled and started to pretend that the fork was a hammer—hammering his eggs and bacon like they were nails on a wall.

My husband then said, "That's not how a fork works."

And my son quickly replied, "Well, you told me to put it to work."

I watched the scene unfold and laughed under my breath. Seeing the fork being used as a hammer was hilarious. Forks were used to eat food, not hit things.

Then I had a sudden thought: How many of God's children were created to be forks, but were working as hammers?

We are each designed differently, and God has a special calling for our individual lives. If we go around doing work to which we have not been called, we will wear ourselves out just like the fork will eventually wear out if used as a hammer.

God is very interested in the large and small aspects of our lives, and He has a purpose for each of us—a purpose that furthers His plan on earth. We can't go around just acting like hammers just because it feels like we are "working" or doing "ministry." We must seek God and hear what He has to say first. Then, if He calls us to the work, He will also prepare us and provide grace, so we can accomplish the task.

God created us. He knows how we can best serve His kingdom. Once we discover who we are in Christ, we can finally find our niche in life and work in a way that best suits us.

But we can never get too comfortable. With every chapter in life, God may change things around a bit. He can transform us into a multi-tool that can be used for different reasons in different seasons—and all for His glory!

Questions: Are you a fork that is doing the work of a hammer? How can you make some changes in your life today that correspond with what God is calling you to? Do you think these changes will help you achieve your work more effectively?

"He has saved us and called us to a holy life—not because of anything we have done but because of his own purpose and grace. This grace was given us in Christ Jesus before the beginning of time" (2 Timothy 1.9 NIV).

Frog or Rock

I woke up early this morning to get some writing done before the day started. Lately, the days have been filled to the brim with activity, leaving me with the dawn, knowing that I'd have at least a few hours alone.

My dachshund, Rusty, realized I was up and came into my office. He sat down and stared at me for a brief moment before barking at me to take him outside. I quickly got up and hushed him to keep his burly voice down. I didn't want the kids to wake up and commence the day too early.

I walked him to the back door and opened it. He hurriedly jumped out, heading for the crisp, green grass. But before he made it off of the cement patio, he began to sniff. I heard a little "ribbit, ribbit." I looked over and saw a frog the size of a Hot Wheels truck, sitting on his haunches and croaking in the early morning.

The frog must have seen Rusty coming his way, because he instantly pushed his entire body down on the ground, closed his eyes and stopped croaking. As Rusty sniffed at him, the frog laid absolutely still. Not a peep could be heard or a single movement could be seen. Since my dog loves to chase things, I was sure he would go after this little frog. But after a few moments of sniffing and waiting, Rusty finally gave up and made his way to the lawn.

I was just about to head back into the house, but I glanced at the frog one last time. I thought maybe I was mistaken. Maybe I hadn't seen a frog after all. I walked over to the frog and stared, as he stayed unmoving on the patio. From a closer view, I could definitely tell that he was a frog, but he almost looked like a rock sitting there.

What a smart frog! Because the frog did not move or croak, Rusty had gotten bored with him and wandered off to do his business. And I realized that this is exactly what we need to do as Christians when we feel like we are being spiritually attacked—stay very still and quiet!

We have an enemy that enjoys making a ruckus in our lives. He would like nothing better than to chase us around and cause us to panic. However, if we simply stay firm on God's Word and His promises, we won't have to run around like crazy people. We can simply close our eyes, lower our voices and wait patiently on the Lord.

"Wait patiently for the LORD. Be brave and courageous. Yes, wait patiently for the LORD" (Psalm 27.14 NLT).

Weight of Presence

I'm entering a new stage of motherhood in life: my youngest child is now almost 7 years old. I can sit in my house without worrying about diapers, baby food and exposed electrical outlets. As I contemplate over that past 11 years of being a mother, there are some incidences that make me laugh.

One such incident happened when my daughter was only about 12 months old. I brought all three kids into the postal store—a feat that caused stress every time. My boys were then about 5 and 3 years old, so taking them to a store with fragile items placed low to the ground had my eyes alert and my body ready to react.

After I finished mailing my item, I gathered up my boys. Thankfully, nothing had been moved or broken. I looked around for my daughter—who had recently learned to walk—but I couldn't find her. I called out her name and began to frantically look around the rows of cards, stationery and other knickknacks, but I did not see her.

My heart began to race. Either she walked outside or someone stole her! I told my boys to come with me. We needed to rush outside to find her. Just when I was about to sprint for the door, my oldest son yelled out, "Mom! I see her!"

"Where is she?" I screamed.

He pointed at me and said, "She's in your arms!"

I looked down and, sure enough, she was right there—on my right hip, tucked securely in the embrace of my right arm. I had gotten so used to the presence of kids in my arms that I no longer noticed their weight. The people in the store watched the entire scene unfold, and they couldn't help but laugh. I laughed too—after my heart rate when back down to normal.

Sometimes we get so used to the presence of God in our lives that we forget He is there. But He says in His Word that He will always be with us, and He will never forsake us. Jesus took our sins, so God's presence could be with us always. If we don't feel God there, maybe we have just grown accustomed to His hand. Maybe we just need someone to point out and say, "He's right there!"

Today, let us take a deeper look at where we see God's hand moving in our lives. He is all around us, providing for us and guiding our steps. We never have to worry about Him leaving us because Jesus reconciled us back to God by His sacrifice on the cross. The Holy Spirit in our lives is proof that Jesus took our sins, so God's presence would be in our lives forever. We just have to trust that He is there.

"Be strong and courageous. Do not be afraid or terrified because of them, for the LORD your God goes with you; he will never leave you nor forsake you" (Deuteronomy 31.6 NIV).

Dream Construction

There is a house near my neighborhood that has been in the process of construction for over three years. This Christmas will mark its third season of empty holidays—no family to fill it, no fireplace to warm it, no Christmas decoration to trim it—completely and utterly alone. But this state of emptiness does not mean that it has been idle. On the contrary, busy hands have been methodically building this home for endless days. The foundation alone took a full year, and the structure of the house took another year!

Every time I pass this house, I'm amazed at what has been accomplished but keenly aware that it is not ready yet. To say this home is a mammoth is an understatement. And to say that it has been hurriedly constructed would be the opposite of the truth. In fact, the design of the house has been well planned and every detail of construction has been scrutinized. The foundation goes deep and the structure of the home is made of steel, not wood. This house is being made to last centuries, not just a single lifetime! But…

I wonder if the family had grown impatient to move in.

I wonder if they have lost hope of ever stepping foot into their dream home.

I wonder if they have visited the construction site to encourage themselves.

As I look at this home, I find understanding for my own impatience, and I'm able to tighten my faith around a deeper hope. Many times, God gives us promises that seem like they will never be fulfilled. We work diligently in obedience to the Holy Spirit and we remain patient to His timing, but after years and years and endless days, we wonder if we will ever step foot into our Promise Land.

We have trouble seeing the finished product, and our hope begins to falter. We want to give up, but the time, energy and resources we have poured into our dream won't allow us to walk away. We wait at the construction site of our dreams, but everything appears dark and desolate. The promise is not yet ready.

And what God keeps reminding me is that the bigger the promise, the more effort and time it will take to build it. God does not build dreams haphazardly, and He wants to build them to last many lifetimes. If His promise to us seems to tarry, we must conclude that the promise is bigger than we had initially expected.

God will build the dream as large and strong as we are willing to wait. The only choice we have then is to cling onto hope as hard and as long as we possibly can. We can't let anything lure us away from the construction site of our dream. If God has given us His YES, we know His promise will come to pass. One day we will step foot into our Promise Land!

So instead of losing hope, we can ask God to give us a divine vision of His promises for our life. We can be in awe of all that He's already accomplished in and through us and not be discouraged by how far we still have to go. The longer we wait, the sweeter the homecoming will be.

We also must be careful not to get sidetracked by other lesser dreams. We might be able to move into these dreams more quickly, but they will only accomplish a fraction of what God can accomplish if we wait on Him. Nothing will ever be more delightful than the plans that God has for us.

Wait on Him. Don't give up. Stay the course. God will turn on the lights of your dream and welcome you home before you know it!

"This vision is for a future time. It describes the end, and it will be fulfilled. If it seems slow in coming, wait patiently, for it will surely take place. It will not be delayed" (Habakkuk 2.3 NLT).

Controlled Step-Up

The New Year is time for getting rid of all those holiday calories. I've been working out all my adult life, and I know that there is nothing much you can do about feasting with family and friends. It is part of the celebration of Christmas, and I'm not going to be a holiday food snob. Although I don't go overboard, I do allow myself about a 3-pound weight gain, which is why I love January 1. It's the time to get the sugar intake under control and lose that extra poundage!

Working out is my favorite way to get back to my preholiday weight. I especially love doing compound exercises that work several muscles at once, including the heart! One exercise that wrecks me every time (in a good way) is the step-up split lunge with weights. This is a highly controlled exercise that uses almost every muscle in the body, including the core to control the body's form.

When watching someone do this exercise, it looks like a piece of cake because the body's form is so controlled. However, when the person finally finishes and drops her weights, she is leaning over and heaving to catch her breath. I find it interesting that such a difficult exercise can look so simple and almost placid, but the controlled movement is important to prevent injury and adequately work the muscles.

This exercise reminds of two types of people.

God allows us to work our faith muscles in order to grow us spiritually. When some people find themselves in a difficult situation, they are controlled and lean heavily on the Lord. They don't complain, and they finish their difficult season with strength and stamina. Other people, however, break their form and flail about injuring themselves and even the people around them. It may look like they are working harder than the ones who are controlled, but in actuality they are not building strength; they are hurting themselves.

Here is the stinger. Which group are we in? Are we the ones who stay strong and controlled, trusting in God, or do we complain and worry, sabotaging the peace around us? Just because someone is making a big fuss doesn't mean her situation is any harder than the person who is standing strong in God. Time will reveal who is relying on the Lord and who is not. One person will walk away a powerhouse of the Holy Spirit and the other a bitter and injured person.

"Not only so, but we also glory in our sufferings, because we know that suffering produces perseverance; perseverance, character; and character, hope. And hope does not put us to shame, because God's love has been poured out into our hearts through the Holy Spirit, who has been given to us" (Romans 5.3-5 NIV).

Simple Musings | Alisa Hope Wagner

Bath Bombs

I was never a bath person. During my twenties, I was too busy working and going to school. And during my thirties, I was too busy keeping up with babies and toddlers. Now that I'm 39 years old, and my youngest child is almost seven, a few of those moment-to-moment demands have slacked off a little. I can ask all three of my kids to read a book and have thirty minutes all to myself!

My forties are looking brighter, and I won't let a few wrinkles get in the way!

I never thought I could create a tranquil spa experience in my own home. My home is a place to be a mother, writer and wife, but it was never a getaway place for relaxation and tranquility—until I looked at that big, empty tub in the middle of my bathroom with fresh eyes!

I dusted off the cobwebs (literally) and purchased a few spa elements—sea salt, essential oils, soaps and the amazing BATH BOMBS! Where have those lovely, balls of explosive awesomeness been all my life?

Since I never experienced a bath bomb before, I didn't know what to expect. I filled the tub, played some relaxing music, grabbed my current book and plunged into bliss! I took the fabulous bath bomb out of its wrapper and read the little label that came with it. I don't recall the exact words of the label, but I remember that it sounded magical.

I gently grasped the bath bomb and tenderly dipped it into the water. Suddenly, the chalky consistency began to fizz and the wonderful ingredients spread into every inch of water in my bath.

As I watched the bath bomb become smaller and permeate the water, I found myself wondering if that is how we infuse with Jesus. We are not meant to simply make room for Him in our lives; rather, we are supposed to allow our entire being dissolve into Him. And once all of our flesh fizzles away, we have now become the likeness of our Savior who is the Living Water!

God created each of us with a beautiful mixture of ingredients that offer a special aroma and balm to the world. When we allow the Living Water to engulf our lives, we become wellsprings of healing tonic to all who are in need.

That's what I want. I want to be used by God for the world. It may mean that the chalky parts of me need to fizzle away, but once I'm saturated with God, I can be used for His great and mighty purposes.

So let's be bath bombs for God. It's not about giving God some space in our lives; it's about letting Him infuse every part of it. How can you let the Living Water infuse your life today?

"Whoever believes in me, as Scripture has said, rivers of living water will flow from within them" (John 7.38 NIV).

Papa Lion

I had a free evening at home after the kids went to sleep. My husband wanted to go for a run, so I asked him to find me something fun to watch on TV before he left. I have "learned incompetence" when it comes to the remote control, so he scrolled through the channels until a lion documentary presented itself.

"Oh, that looks interesting," I said. It was only about 40 minutes long, so I figured it would be done before he got home. Plus, I could learn a little something while I relaxed.

As the show continued, I was introduced to a pride of lions. There was a daddy lion, three mamas and a whole bunch of cubs. I enjoyed getting to know each lion and his/her respective place in the pride.

The little cubs of the pride were able to play, watch and learn as much as they could. They didn't make their first kill until about two years old, so the rest of the time they experienced crazy, little antics of trial and error.

The mamas, however, did a lot of work. Not only did they all take turns nursing, protecting and teaching the young cubs, they also made all the kills for the entire family. All three of mamas worked together to bring down the zebra or warthog in an amazing display of teamwork and strength.

As the show progressed, I became a little put out by the daddy lion.

He seemed to lie around all day, play with the kids a little and, when the mamas made their kill, he went straight over and had his fill first. He wouldn't let anyone touch the kill that the mamas brought down until he was full. He was a massive beast, eating so much meat that I wondered if anything would be left for the rest of the pride.

I thought to myself, "That's not fair. The mamas take care of the young and hunt for all the food. What does that daddy do besides make more babies?"

That's what I was thinking until two predator lions came close to the pride. The narrator said that if the predators attacked the pride and won, they would try to kill all the babies and the family would be destroyed.

Suddenly, lazy daddy lion turned into fierce papa lion, protecting his family. The daddy lion didn't bat an eye. While the mamas stayed with the young, he ran full force toward the two predators and attacked them. I had never seen something so hauntingly awesome. He roared and thrashed his giant claws at the enemy. His massive size and strength were no comparison, and after only a few minutes, the two predator lions ran off.

When the daddy lion won the fight, the entire pride roared a warning to all that could hear. If they could speak, I know what they would be shouting: "Stay away from our family, you enemies!"

That's when it hit me.

During all that time, the daddy was eating and relaxing, he was preparing for the moment that the enemy would confront his family. He was well fed, strong and ready to protect what was entrusted to him.

"For the husband is the head of the wife as Christ is the head of the church, his body, of which he is the Savior" (Ephesians 5.23 NIV).

Although human families are different from lion prides, there is a valuable lesson to be learned here. The man of the family is called to lead and protect those entrusted to him, and the Devil will always target him first. The predator walks around like a lion, waiting for the right moment to attack. As a wife, I don't fully comprehend the weight my husband feels as the head of the family, but I can strengthen him and provide for his needs. This way he will be fully rested and empowered to fight the predators when they come to attack our marriage and our family.

There is a spiritual battle waged against our families, and Satan wants to rip them apart. God designed the family, so Satan hates them. If wives and husbands strengthen and encourage each other in their different duties and roles, we will all be able to do our part in protecting the sanctity of our homes.

"Be alert and of sober mind. Your enemy the devil prowls around like a roaring lion looking for someone to devour" (1 Peter 5.8 NIV).

Coral Cliff

For Spring Break, our family went on a Caribbean cruise. Just recently have our kids been old enough to appreciate such an international trip. One of the stops on the itinerary was the island of Roatan, which is part of Honduras. We had a snorkeling excursion scheduled, and I couldn't wait to float over the coral reef in that area.

Right away, my seven-year-old daughter did not want to snorkel, so I told my husband to go with our boys without me. Although I wanted to have the snorkeling experience, I was content to lie on the beach and watch my daughter pick up seashells.

After an hour, my husband and middle son decided that they were done snorkeling, so they met me back at the beach. However, our oldest son (11 years old) wanted to keep snorkeling, so I decided to grab my gear and join him. My husband was happy to chill on one of the beach chairs and bask in the sun.

I met my son in the water, and we floated together, following a rope that led through the coral reef. Never before had I seen so many amazing colored fish. Everyone was vibrantly painted, and I couldn't help but be amazed at the creativity of our God.

As I followed my son in awe of the colorful world beneath me, the coral reef dropped off at least 125 feet. To a person who has a fear of heights, the sight of the coral cliff falling away into a dark blue abyss was alarming. Instantly, I felt my chest tighten. My son kept floating forward over the deep descent, and all I could think of was getting him out of that water and back onto the beach.

I felt the Lord's presence reminding me that I would not fall because the water around me carried me—as long as I worked with it to stay afloat. Although the situation looked scary and impossible, I was safe in the water's embrace.

"For we live by faith, not by sight" (2 Corinthians 5.7 NIV).

Many times, God leads us into impossible and scary situations. If we "swim" by sight alone, we will never make it because fear will cause us to retreat. But if we "swim" by faith, we will see God's presence all around us, carrying us through the impossible situation. The only way we will learn to float over impossibility is if we put all our trust into God. If He says we can do it, He will provide a way. We just have to have more faith in His promises rather than the scary situation that our eyes see.

"Jesus looked at them intently and said, 'Humanly speaking, it is impossible. But with God everything is possible'" (Matthew 19.26 NLT).

My writing and I have moved into my new home—my new website! You can now find me at www.alisahopewagner.com. It feels so roomy, and I can't wait to spread out and get comfortable. I can post blogs, daily devotionals and vlogs (video blogs) all at the SAME time! I don't know, but I may get carried away a bit. Just don't get me started!

As I was thinking about moving into a bigger space, I realized that—unlike physical houses—websites aren't real in a tangible sense. There is nothing tangible about them. In fact, my highly analytical 11-year-old son reminds me all the time that the Internet is just full of ones and zeros. I may have a lot of writing, images and links on my new site, but nothing is tangible. It's all an awareness of the mind. But all my thinking, musing, wondering and writing must have some kind of existence, right?

I know that although I've spent thousands of hours typing a bunch of ones and zeros into a space that doesn't actually exist, I have done the following: 1) grown spiritually, 2) discovered seeds of faith, 3) wrestled with my flesh, 4) made a bunch of mistakes, 5) forged many breakthroughs, 6) drawn closer to Jesus, and 7) stayed faithful to God's call. A bunch of ones and zeros have sure had a profound effect on my life! Ten years ago, I started blogging out of obedience never realizing how God would shape my faith through my persistent pecks at the keyboard.

Many of the most important things in life are not tangible....they are all an awareness of the mind, the heart and the spirit. They are the products of God's presence in our lives, and they cannot be bought or sold, but they can be ATTAINED!

"But the Holy Spirit produces this kind of fruit in our lives: love, joy, peace, patience, kindness, goodness, faithfulness, gentleness, and self-control. There is no law against these things!" (Galatians 5.22-23 NLT).

And that is what I want to expand upon on my beautifully designed website made up of talent, effort, prayer and, yes, ones and zeros. I want to expand my awareness of my Father God, His goodness to me and my place in His plan. The Creator who designed this earth with all its lands, seas, plants, animals and people may not be tangible, but He is alive and well on this earth and in my heart.

I want to grow my awareness of Him. I want to take my mind off of my problems, my shortcomings, my desires and my wants and become mindful, heartful and soulful of a God who would willingly dip His Spirit into tattered flesh, so He could bring me back into relationship with Him. I want to apprehend His movements in my life. I want to sense His voice in my spirit. I want to feel His presence by my side. Every day is one day in His courts, every day is heaven on earth—if I could only perceive it.

I may not be able to wrap my fingers around God, but I can wrap my life around Him.

"Indeed these are the mere edges of His ways, And how small a whisper we hear of Him! But the thunder of His power who can understand?" (Job 26.14 NKJV).

Five-Year Journey

My husband and I went to the grocery store on our way home from our date night, and guess what I found on one of those Christian book/devotional kiosks? A devotional prayer book that showcased many of my writings! It was my very first paid publication when I began using my writing to share Christ's love with others. I wrote for the publisher of the book in 2010, but I didn't find out the books were published until 2013. I never checked. I figured that maybe the books didn't come to fruition—a common occurrence in the publishing world.

However, years later after I contributed my writing, a sweet young lady messaged me at my Facebook Author Page, and let me know how much she appreciated the book and my writing. What a surprise! I had no idea what she was talking about and it took several comments back and forth for me to figure it out. The prayer book that I had believed was a no-go had been indeed published in 2011. And somehow it made a journey from the publisher's location in Illinois all the way south to my town of Corpus Christi, Texas!

One hour before I found the prayer book, I had just been at our local bookstore with my husband, complaining to God that my books were not on any of the bookshelves. All the while one of my books (about hope!) was just beyond the freezer section and behind the flower section of my local supermarket! God was reminding me that His ways are greater than my ways and His thoughts are greater than my thoughts (ref. Isaiah 55.8-9). Not everyone frequents the local bookstore, but EVERYONE has to get groceries. I couldn't help feeling overwhelmed with the sense that God is always in control.

It may take over five years to see the fruit of our work dedicated to Him, but He doesn't forget a single act of obedience. God has the universe at His disposal. With a wave of a hand, He can make our work turn up anywhere—even late Sunday night while out getting groceries for the week. I know it may seem small, but I was enamored with God's mercy, knowing that He always has my best interest in mind. He wants to incorporate my life into His greater plan, so I need to listen closely to His voice and follow His leading. If I don't see results right away, I can trust that at any moment when I least expect it, God will reveal how little parts of my obedience are forming His Kingdom here on earth and for eternity!

"Now when He was asked by the Pharisees when the kingdom of God would come, He answered them and said, 'The kingdom of God does not come with observation; nor will they say, "See here!" or "See there!" For indeed, the kingdom of God is within you'" (Luke 17.20-21 NKJV).

Self-Harm of Words

Self-mutilation, self-injury and self-harm—these are the words that describe a condition of a person who purposefully hurts him/herself. Whenever we experience first-hand someone struggling with self-harm, we can't believe our eyes. The evidence of self-hurt is caught in grotesque images of cuts, burns and bruises. People struggling with this condition willfully hurt themselves because of a condition in the heart.

It's interesting that we instantly seek help for people struggling with physical self-harm, but every day we experience emotional self-harm and think nothing of it. We speak negative words over ourselves, and we believe this is normal or even okay. But negative self-talk is not okay. We damage God's beautiful creation with every word that cuts, burns and bruises our hearts and souls.

I struggle with negative self-talk, and I think (if women were honest) many of us do. We want to be thinner, prettier, smarter, more talented, funnier and more adventurous. We examine our flaws with a microscope and purposefully ignore God's thoughts of truth about us. We self-mutilate with every piercing thought and word and wonder why we can't find joy in our day. But what we don't realize is that emotional self-harm is a condition of the heart too. We have forgotten what our Heavenly

Father says about us, and we have listened to and believed the lies of the enemy.

Today, we need to stop the negative self-talk—even little mean words can chip away at our joy. We must start each day with a fresh revelation of how God sees us. Our emotions need to be set in truth from the get-go and surrendered to the authority of the Holy Spirit. God sees us as His sons and daughters. He values us and places His worth in each of us. He has an amazing plan for our lives.

He has invested His Son, Jesus Christ, into our hearts and souls. We can't let the enemy and our negative self-talk steal what Jesus died to give us—His righteousness, His forgiveness, His grace and His victory. Let us recall and reclaim God's precious thoughts over us, so we can experience joy every day, not just when we feel like it!

"How precious also are Your thoughts to me, O God! How great is the sum of them! If I should count them, they would be more in number than the sand; When I awake, I am still with You" (Psalm 139.17-18 NKJV).

You are VICTORIOUS: "No, in all these things we are more than conquerors through him who loved us" (Romans 8.37 NIV).

You are RIGHTEOUS: "And to put on the new self, created to be like God in true righteousness and holiness" (Ephesians 4.24 NIV).

You are ROYALTY: "But you are a chosen people, a royal priesthood, a holy nation, God's special possession, that you may declare the praises of him who called you out of darkness into his wonderful light" (1 Peter 2.9 NIV).

You are NEW: "Therefore, if anyone is in Christ, he is a new creation. The old has gone, the new has come" (2 Corinthians 5.17 NKJV).

You have PURPOSE: "For we are God's handiwork, created in Christ Jesus to do good works, which God prepared in advance for us to do" (Ephesians 2.10 NIV).

You have LIGHT: "You are all children of the light and children of the day. We do not belong to the night or to the darkness" (1 Thessalonians 5.5 NIV).

You have a GEAT FUTURE: "For I know the thoughts that I think toward you, says the Lord, thoughts of peace and not of evil, to give you a future and a hope" (Jeremiah 29.11 NKJV).

You SHINE: "…Then you will shine among them like stars in the sky…" (Philippians 2.15 NIV).

You are GOD'S CHILD: "Now if we are children, then we are heirs—heirs of God and co-heirs with Christ. If indeed we share in His sufferings in order that we may also share with His glory" (Romans 8.17 NIV).

Take CAPTIVE every thought that harms your image in Christ. Those arguments of negative self-talk are LIES, and they need to be demolished! Today, how can you make your thoughts stay obedient to Christ?

"We demolish arguments and every pretension that sets itself up against the knowledge of God, and we take captive every thought to make it obedient to Christ" (2 Corinthians 10.5 NIV).

Call Her Blessed

"But he said to me, 'My grace is sufficient for you, for my power is made perfect in weakness.' Therefore, I will boast all the more gladly about my weaknesses, so that Christ's power may rest on me" (2 Corinthians 12.9 NIV).

Motherhood has a great way of reminding us of all our little human imperfections. Every day there is at least one little person in our lives who has an up-close encounter with our flaws, mistakes and struggles. It's easy to become discouraged if perfection is our goal. But perfection can't be our purpose as mothers because it will only set us up for failure. Our children won't have a perfect mom, but they can have a mom who receives grace with mercy.

When our children become aware of our mistakes, they also need to become aware of how we accept grace. We can say sorry easily and accept our imperfections without getting discouraged, knowing that Jesus Christ more than compensates for our mess-ups. We can be a standard to our children of how to receive grace with mercy. We can accept our struggle without giving up or feeling defeated. We can get up gracefully after a fall, dust ourselves off and walk in confidence of the Cross once more.

Our children can watch our efforts to walk by faith in Christlikeness, keenly mindful that we become stronger with every struggle, increasingly faithful through every failure and victorious in every obstacle we overcome. They need to see us move in grace, so they won't be haunted with the elusive idea of perfection. And as they experience us leaning into God with every battle that beats us down, they will learn how to reach for Him in their own time of need.

Our children may never stand up and call us "perfect," but they can stand up and call us "blessed." We are blessed when we openly live in the redemption of Jesus Christ on a daily basis. We can boast in the weaknesses that motherhood exposes, so we can rely on Christ's power as mothers. And our children will be thankful that we taught them how to receive grace with mercy! One day they will arise and call us BLESSED!

"Her children arise and call her blessed..." (Proverbs 31.28 NIV).

Return to Confidence

"This is what the Sovereign LORD, the Holy One of Israel, says: 'Only in returning to me and resting in me will you be saved. In quietness and confidence is your strength. But you will have none of it'" (Isaiah 30.15 NLT).

Return. Rest. Quiet. Confidence. These four words are many times extremely difficult for us to live out, especially when we are confronted with a struggle. But the truth is that all of us have struggles. Even though each person's struggle may seem different on the outside, the core of each one is simple: there is something happening that we don't like. And instead of resting in God's authority and strength, we try to fix the situation in our limited human ability. But there are just some things that are out of our control.

Yes, God wants us to use the mind and imagination He has gifted us to influence circumstances according to His will. However, He allows us to enter storms that we can't change, fix or make disappear. And in these situations, we must Return to God, Rest in His sovereignty, remain Quiet in His strength, and have Confidence in His will. It is a scary proposition this "letting go of control," but it is so freeing. Knowing that there is absolutely nothing we can do to solve the problem forces us to make a choice. We can either allow worry to strangle our peace and joy or we can reach outside of ourselves for a supernatural peace and joy that is only found in God.

During the prophetic ministry of Isaiah, God's people were confronted with the same choice. Sadly, they chose to try to fix the problem themselves, which concluded in their ultimate destruction. God allows both good and evil to bring the fruition of His plan on earth, and we need to accept both as they come. We do not live in a perfect world, but we do have a perfect God. He does not let a single tear to be shed unnoticed. He sees everything, and He will shine His glory in our broken world. But we have to trust Him.

"You keep track of all my sorrows. You have collected all my tears in your bottle. You have recorded each one in your book" (Psalm 56.8 NLT).

We can take God at His Word. When we Return, Rest and remain Quiet and Confident before Him, He may not save the situation, but He does promise to save us. No matter what is happening in this world, we can rest assured that as Christ-followers we will have eternal life in heaven with God. Regardless of how gray and dreary this life becomes, we can have peace that we will dwell with God forever. And just that truth should give every cloudy day a silver lining. We remain safe and secure in the palm of God's hand, and nothing and no one can force us away from His presence.

"I give them eternal life, and they shall never perish; no one will snatch them out of my hand" (John 10.28 NIV).

My family and I went on a summer vacation, and one tourist attraction on my list to visit was a coffee farm. We found a locally owned café and coffee farm located on several acres of beautifully lined coffee trees. When I asked if we could have a tour, a friendly barista quickly took off her apron and ushered us passed the buffet of chocolate-covered coffee beans and through the backdoor of the shop.

As we entered the wonderful landscape beyond the café, I could instantly smell the sweet aroma of the little white buds that dotted the coffee trees. The barista was surprised by the number of flowers speckling the green clusters of unripe coffee cherries. The white flowers only bloom for a few days before the fruit appears. Coffee beans are not beans at all. Rather, they are the pits of the ripe, red fruit called the cherry that spring up once the flower withers. The red fruit is edible, but these cherries still had a few months left of ripening.

The barista explained many details of the coffee tree, answering all of my kids' questions and a few of my own. My mind went to the investment involved growing all of the trees, so I asked how long it took until the trees produced their first crop. The young woman answered that it could take the coffee tree up to seven years to produce its first fruit. Wow! That was a long time to wait for an investment to start paying off. But the young woman added that once the coffee tree started growing useable fruit, the tree could produce for up to 100 years.

I thought of the scripture that describes sowing and reaping. We can sow thousands of seeds in a certain field and become impatient when our work brings no fruit. We may be tempted to think that God has been false in His Word, and that the promise of sowing and reaping is untrue. Instead of becoming bitter, however, we need to trust as the café owner must have trusted. He knew that his acres of coffee trees would produce eventually. He simply had to wait year after year for his trees to mature. The wait would be worth it, though. Once his trees produced, they would offer their fruit to him, his kids and his grandkids!

Many times, it takes years for our promises to mature. If we have sown according to the Holy Spirit, we will eventually see the fruit. If we sowed generously, we will receive a generous return for our investment. Even though our circumstances suggest that our trees of effort are barren, we must trust that God's Word stands true. A crop will come out of our obedience. We simply need to rest in God and allow Him to bless our land in His timing, trusting that many generations will be blessed by our faithfulness.

"Remember this: Whoever sows sparingly will also reap sparingly, and whoever sows generously will also reap generously" (2 Corinthians 9.6 NIV).

Cube Algorithm

After weeks of effort, my 12-year-old son completed the Rubik's Cube. The fact that he even wanted to engage in this challenge blows my mind. As a child, the Rubik's Cube was an impossibility for me. Even with my vibrant imagination, I could not conceive of a reality where I would ever figure out the Rubik's mystery. The more I slid the colored cubes around, the more I messed up the color patterns.

I remember one time I figured out one side of the Rubik's Cube and stopped there. Every time I tried to complete another color pattern, I would rearrange my finished side. I decided that I did not want to risk losing my one completed side to solve the other five. I didn't realize that in order to achieve the color pattern for all six sides, the Rubik's Cube would first have to go through disorder.

My son explained that cracking the code is not about focusing on the color pattern, but rather on the algorithms of all the turns. An algorithm is a process or set of rules to be followed to solve a problem. Focusing on the color pattern will only lead to defeat, but focusing on the movement of each turn will lead to victory. There is a process that can be employed to complete every Rubik's Cube. It's not a mystery at all. In fact, if the algorithm is followed, anyone can solve the Rubik's Cube. It may seem disorderly at first, but—color-by-color and side-by-side—the Rubik's Cube will fall into place.

The same is true for our lives. God has an algorithm for victory that is found in His Word and His will. On the surface, this algorithm may seem to disorder the pieces we have tried so hard to arrange, but we have to trust the process. We must close our eyes and stop looking at the reality of things and begin to see with eyes of faith. God is moving the pieces of our lives, and with every turn we transform into His beautiful design. His movements may not make sense to us now, but eventually they will fall into place. If we can stay faithful to the process, God will arrange our lives for our good, our future and our hope.

Do you feel like God is rearranging your life? Will you trust God and His movements? Have faith in God's algorithm for your life and watch how beautiful it becomes!

"'For I know the plans I have for you,' says the Lord. 'They are plans for good and not for disaster, to give you a future and a hope'" (Jeremiah 29.11 NLT).

New Crop

I live next to acres of farmland. Every harvesting season, I'm so excited to watch the giant harvester machines gather all the grain. The tiny seeds that were planted that spring have now become large crops of produce, and the farmers set out to reap the results of their hard work. I wonder how good it must feel to finally fill the storehouses with the "fruits" of the farmers' labor.

After the difficult task of harvesting is finished and the crop is safely dispersed, the fields look rather pathetic. The remaining chopped and twisted stalks look like rows of defeated soldiers coming in from a devastating battle. The acres of farmland make for a tattered and disheveled landscape, unfolding against the beautiful, sunlit horizon. It's almost depressing to behold, and I have to remind myself that there will be new life in the death of that year's crop.

Finally, the tractors come in and till the earth. The yellowed and ragged stalks are mixed in with the earth, and the dark brown soil appears like a clean slate along the skyline. Possibility, new beginnings, fresh start – are all words that come to mind when I see the acres of empty fields. And I know that the dilapidated stalks will become nourishment for next year's harvest.

Sometimes God allows acres of our life to be plowed over. Whatever crop we produced is taken away, and we feel like we are left with nothing but tattered dreams and shredded efforts. But God will not allow the fields of our obedience to stay desolate. He will gently till the earth of our hearts, mixing the brokenness with the richness of His favor, blessing, and purpose. Our past will become the fertilizer for our future.

God may destroy the small crop we are clinging onto now in order to give us a bigger and better one. This process doesn't feel good, and we will feel like defeated soldiers coming in from a devastating battle, but we can trust that God knows what He is doing. He will use all things for our good and for His great plan. Nothing in our life – our effort, our heartbreak, or faithfulness—is ever wasted. God will use our brokenness to enrich our lives and the lives of others.

"I will plant trees in the barren desert—
cedar, acacia, myrtle, olive, cypress, fir, and pine.
I am doing this so all who see this miracle
will understand what it means—
that it is the Lord who has done this,
the Holy One of Israel who created it."
- (Isaiah 41.19-20 NLT)

Thunder Follows Rain

"He is a voice shouting in the wilderness, "Prepare the way for the LORD's coming! Clear the road for him!'" (Mark 1.3 NLT).

"What's wrong, Sweetie? Did the thunder wake you?" I asked my daughter, barely able to open my eyelids. I lifted my hand toward her face and stroked her cheek and her long chestnut hair.

"Yes, Mommy," she whimpered. "The thunder is scary."

I demanded my eyes awake and slipped out of my warm bed. I lifted my daughter and wrapped her legs around my waist, and she stretched her arms around my neck. I walked through the dark house to her bedroom. I could hear the thunder in the distance and see the flashes of lightning in the kitchen window.

When I got to her bed, I gently folded her back under the covers. I knelt on the carpet, placed my elbows on the edge of the bed and started petting her face.

"Now, it's time to go to bed. The thunder isn't scary. It can't hurt you."

"But it's loud, and I can't sleep," my daughter whispered. I could see her eyes wide in the glow of the nightlight she turns on at bedtime every night.

"You don't have to be scared of thunder," I began. I felt so tired and desperately wanted to go back to bed, but I knew that I needed to calm her fears.

I thought quickly. "Did you know that Thunder is best friends with Rain?" I began.

She shook her head. "No, I didn't know that."

"Yes," I nodded. "Thunder loves Rain, so it always announces when Rain is coming."

"Really?" she asked.

"They have been friends for a very long time. Thunder loves to let everyone know when Rain is on the way. Thunder can't water the grass or fill up the lakes, but it can tell everyone when its friend will come. It has a booming voice that echoes across the sky, so everyone can be ready for when Rain arrives," I said.

My daughter stared at me, and I could see images forming in her young mind.

I continued. "Some people don't like Thunder. They think it's loud, and it wakes them up while they are sleeping in their warm beds. They feel safe in their homes, and they don't care if Rain is coming. Thunder irritates them or even frightens them. But other people love Thunder. These people need the rain. They are farmers and ranchers who must have Rain to feed their crops and their animals."

My daughter listened intently.

I stopped. "But you know what?" I asked.

"What," she whispered.

"We all need Rain. Nothing on this earth would survive without Rain's help. We should all be thankful to hear the roar of Thunder making the way for Rain. Thunder is not a nuisance. It's a blessing," I finished.

My daughter thought for a moment and repeated my final statement. "It's a blessing."

"It is," I agreed. "Do you like that story about Thunder and Rain?" I asked.

She nodded her head and smiled. Just then the thunder bellowed in the distance.

"It looks like Rain is on its way," I said.

"It's on the way to feed the plants and animals," she said, as she closed her eyes. "Thunder is just letting me know."

I watched my daughter fall asleep before I made my way back to my room.

I thought about Thunder and Rain, and the spiritual implications they present. I know John the Baptist was like Thunder, making the way for the Lord. Many people didn't like John the Baptist. He irritated and scared people. But those desperate for the Rain loved his voice. They flocked into the dry wilderness looking for Living Water.

I thought about my own life. My writing is like Thunder too. I proclaim Jesus on every page. My words may irritate or even scare people, but I know someday they will find themselves desperate for Jesus. The security of their homes and beds will be compromised, and they will see their need for a Savior. They will come to the sound of my thunder, seeking the life-giving Rain in my writing.

"But those who drink the water I give will never be thirsty again. It becomes a fresh, bubbling spring within them, giving them eternal life" (John 4.14 NLT).

Sprinkler System

A section of our sprinkler system stopped working, so a patch of our lawn did not get watered all summer long. We live in South Texas, and the southern heat dried up that patch of grass, leaving it sickly yellow and dead.

One day my daughter went up to the dead grass and started tugging chunks of it out of the ground. "Look, Mommy," she said. "The yellow grass is easy to pull out of the ground."

I was intrigued. I went to the dead grass, grabbed a handful and sure enough the entire clump came out easily. I reached for a section of thick, green grass next to the dead patch and yanked on it. The healthy blades of grass stayed strong and the roots held on tight. The lush grass wouldn't even budge.

As I looked at the green and yellow grass, I uncovered one of Satan's schemes. He knows we aren't easily moved when our "sprinkler system" from heaven is running fine, and God's Word and Voice are able to water us daily. Instead of tempting us right away, Satan will just try to sabotage our flow from the Lord by distracting us from drinking from His Living Water.

"The Spirit and the bride say, 'Come!' And let the one who hears say, 'Come!' Let the one who is thirsty come; and let the one who wishes take the free gift of the water of life." (Revelation 22.17 NIV).

After a few months of spiritual drought, we become weakened prey for Satan to destroy. Our blades have shriveled and our roots are dead, so any temptation Satan throws our way will knock us down and pull us right out of God's will.

Temptation is a part of life, but we don't have to fear it when we are strong in the Lord. The real problem comes slowly and quietly. Distraction from spending time with God and His Word will cause us to be easy targets. We could easily walk away from our family, witness, ministry and destiny with one simple tug from the enemy.

Let us never cease spending time with God and consuming resources that speak His heart. In this way, we will be strong in the Lord to resist all kinds of temptation.

"They are like trees planted along the riverbank,
bearing fruit each season.
Their leaves never wither,
and they prosper in all they do" (Psalm 1.3 NLT).

Enhanced Soup

Every morning, I read a devotional with my kids during breakfast. We have a large collection of devotional books in a drawer of the kitchen curio cabinet, including some of my own.

One morning we read a devotional that I had written years ago about Elisha and the poisoned pot of soup (2 Kings 4.38-41.) One of the prophets had picked poisonous gourds, cut them up and mixed them into the soup. When Elisha discovered the soup was poisoned, he threw a handful of flour into the pot, and the toxic stew became a pleasing meal for the prophets.

After we read the story, I compared Jesus to being the Bread of Life. Jesus is like the flour being mixed into our lives—neutralizing the poison of sin, so we can be pleasing to God.

"God is pleased with us because He sees His Son, Jesus, in us," I explained. "Jesus took all of our sins on the cross, and now we are perfect before a Holy God."

My analytical 12-year old son thought for a moment. "If God sees Jesus in me, is there room for God to see me too?" he asked.

I've thought of this question many times. If God is pleased with us because He sees His Son in us, how does our unique personality fit into the mix? I've struggled to explain that Jesus infuses our own personality, soul and design with His presence, making us perfect and whole. But it has always been a difficult truth to explain without a concrete image to go with it.

Suddenly, I saw the image of the soup in my mind.

The soup was a unique mixture of ingredients used to feed the hungry prophets during a regional famine that year. The broth had its own flavor and texture that would never be replicated exactly the same again. And when the flour was mixed in, the soup didn't become something different. It simply stayed itself but better—healthier, richer and toxin-free.

Finally, I had an image to give my son.

I explained that we are each a unique soup that God has prepared during this time for a special purpose. When Jesus saves us, we still have the same ingredients in us that we were born with, but now we are healthier, richer (in mind, body and spirit) and sin free. And God can use us to bless the people and world around us.

Jesus infuses every single cell of our body, mind and spirit, purging all the sin that makes us poisonous. God is able to have a relationship with us through the Finished Work of Jesus on the Cross, and we are redeemed from poison the enemy has tried to cook into our lives. No matter what we have done or what has been done to us, we can be used for the great purposes God has for us.

Jesus doesn't stifle our individuality. He enhances and perfects it.

"Then Christ will make his home in your hearts as you trust in him. Your roots will grow down into God's love and keep you strong. And may you have the power to understand, as all God's people should, how wide, how long, how high, and how deep his love is. May you experience the love of Christ, though it is too great to understand fully. Then you will be made complete with all the fullness of life and power that comes from God" (Ephesians 3.17-19 NLT).

Pressure Holes

There is a lot of construction taking place near my home. When I leave our subdivision, whether I go right or left, there are great machines digging, drilling and moving materials around. One day as I was driving into town, I saw a large contraption drilling holes into a massive, misshapen block of cement. The cement slab was part of the old road, and the machine was breaking it down for removal.

I found it interesting that the machine drilled holes into the cement first before applying pressure. Once there were several holes about one foot apart from each other, the machine's clamps bore down on the cement, crumbling it into chunks.

Both the holes and the pressure were necessary to tear down the strong block of cement.

Satan knows this is true for God's children too. The Bible guarantees that we will have great pressures and troubles in this life (John 16.33). The holidays are definitely proof of this truth. Christmas can bring amazing joy, but it also may add great amounts of financial, emotional, relational and mental pressures that are intensified with the busyness of the season. This is the time that we need to make sure that we are filling our weak areas with God's grace. Are we staying in God's Word? Are we communicating with our Heavenly Father? Are we renewing our minds in Christ daily? Are we finding rest in the Holy Spirit's strength?

Satan wants nothing more than to crumble us to bits, stealing our joy and robbing us of special moments. He wants to watch us fall and make the lives of those around us miserable. But no matter the pressure Satan places on our lives, if we are fortified in Christ, no amount of force can break us. Our relationship with God not only offers us limitless peace, joy and love, but it also protects us from breaking when we are weak.

When our lives are completely surrendered to God, we can trust that His strength is made perfect in us, especially in our "pressures holes" (2 Corinthians 12.9). No matter the circumstance and the pressures surrounding it, we can trust that God will give us strength to continue each day with joy and peace.

"I can do all things [which He has called me to do] through Him who strengthens and empowers me [to fulfill His purpose—I am self-sufficient in Christ's sufficiency; I am ready for anything and equal to anything through Him who infuses me with inner strength and confident peace]" (Philippians 4.13 AMP).

Ten Days

"Daniel then said to the guard whom the chief official had appointed over Daniel, Hananiah, Mishael and Azariah, 'Please test your servants for ten days: Give us nothing but vegetables to eat and water to drink. Then compare our appearance with that of the young men who eat the royal food, and treat your servants in accordance with what you see.' So he agreed to this and tested them for ten days" (Daniel 1.11-14 NIV).

Many times, God wants to make a change in our lives. We can sense the change, but we don't have the full vision of what God wants to accomplish. Since we can't see the end result, it is difficult to make the strenuous steps towards change. Change is hard—no matter how good it is for us. But there is a way to get a glimpse of the power behind this change.

We can follow Daniel's lead and take the 10-day challenge. Daniel replaced royal food with vegetables and examined to see whether this change had benefits or not. At the end of his 10 days, Daniel was 10 times better than all the rest of his peers!

The 10-day challenge is an easy gauge that will help us better see what God is trying to do in our lives. And once we commit to doing our change for 10 days and see the amazing results, the total transfer of habits will be easier to accomplish because we can finally grasp God's bigger plan. We can do as Daniel did and test what the Holy Spirit is trying to accomplish in us, trusting that God always has our good in mind.

- First, pick a start and end date, making sure 10 full days will transpire.

- Second, make the transfer and replace a lesser habit with a better one.

- Third, watch as the 10 days unfold and see how your life is better as a result.

For example, replace drinking soda with drinking hot tea for 10 days. Replace an hour of TV time with an hour walk for 10 days. Replace complaining about work with rejoicing about work for 10 days. Replace speaking the negative with speaking the positive by faith for 10 days. Replace harboring unforgiveness with offering forgiveness for 10 days. Replace listening to the news with listening to inspirational podcasts for 10 days. Or replace flipping through Facebook to flipping through your Bible app for 10 days.

Make the change for 10 full days, and then look at your life and see how different one small transfer of habits can make. God will bless your faith. He only wants to make this change because He has something better for you in mind. Trust that God knows what He is doing. He sees what we cannot see, and His ways are higher than ours (Isaiah 55.8-9). We may not fully understand the larger vision of God's movements on earth, but we can get a small preview in the 10-day challenge to help us stay aligned with His Kingdom Plan.

"The king talked with them, and he found none equal to Daniel, Hananiah, Mishael and Azariah; so they entered the king's service. In every matter of wisdom and understanding about which the king questioned them, he found them ten times better than all the magicians and enchanters in his whole kingdom" (Daniel 1.19-20 NIV).

My son has been playing piano since he was four years old. Now at age 12, he is very good at playing solo music. He has an amazing gift of listening to music and finding the keys by hearing. Whenever he plays a song, he memorizes the music first. This can be a good thing because he can play music without having the notes in front of him. But it can be a bad thing because he reads music slowly since he leans so heavily on his hearing. He can't just sit down with a piece of music and play each note. He has to study each note first, memorize their order and then play the song.

This happens a lot with piano players since much of their study is done alone. In order for my son to get better at reading music, he tried out for our local youth symphony. He made the string ensemble, but the maestro understood that although my son plays very well, his music reading is slow. My son will have to work on reading each note as he plays them and develops that skill.

At the first rehearsal, my son felt lost. Not only had he never played with other instruments before, he also fell behind in playing the music. He couldn't read the notes nearly as quickly as the other students playing violin and cello who had learned to play their instruments among the orchestra. My son who excels in solo playing appeared disoriented and slow. Although he has been playing piano for 7 years, his talent did not show as he played with the ensemble. It was like he was starting from scratch again. I have total confidence that he will learn quickly. He has so much strength in piano playing that I trust this weakness will not last long.

Many times, our faith is solid, but we have relied on certain developed strengths, and God wants to improve weaker areas of our lives. God puts us in a situation where we feel insecure and lost. The people around us can't see our strengths because the new circumstances only highlight our lack. We may want to retreat from the situation and save ourselves from being humbled. However, if we stick with it, God will bless us with greater ability and influence. He may humble us for the moment, but He will eventually lift us back up. If our faith is strong, we will grow and learn quickly. It may be difficult to start from scratch again, but God knows that our exposed weakness will strengthen rapidly. And pretty soon, we'll be able to handle a vast variety of situations, so we can be used by God to reach a larger platform.

"Humble yourselves before the Lord, and he will lift you up" (James 4.10 NIV).

The Fig Tree

We all come to a time in our lives where we are confronted with a choice: Will we put our faith in our natural circumstances or will we put our faith in God's promises?

Peter had this choice. Would he walk on water or would he sink? Which was more powerful to him: The Word from Jesus or the winds and the waves?

"He [Jesus] said, 'Come,' So Peter got out of the boat and walked on the water and came to Jesus. But when he saw the wind, he was afraid, and beginning to sink he cried out, 'Lord, save me'" (Matthew 14.29-30 ESV).

The Israelites also had this choice. Would they walk into their Promised Land that God had given them or would they run away in fear? Which was more powerful to them: The Word from God or the giants living in their land?

"The LORD said to Moses, 'Send men to explore Canaan, which I'm giving to the Israelites. Send one leader from each of their ancestors' tribes" (Numbers 13.1-2 ESV).

"Caleb told the people to be quiet and listen to Moses. Caleb said, 'Let's go now and take possession of the land. We should be more than able to conquer it.' But the men who had gone with him said, "We can't attack those people! They're too strong for us!'" (Numbers 13.30-31 ESV).

Jesus walking with His disciples noticed a fig tree filled with leaves. He walked straight to that fig tree expecting fruit; however, no fruit was there because it wasn't the season for fruit.

"And seeing in the distance a fig tree in leaf, he went to see if he could find anything on it. When He came to it, he found nothing but leaves, for it was not the season for figs. And he said to it, 'May no one ever eat fruit from you again'" (Mark 11.13-14 ESV).

The fig tree had this choice. Would it bear fruit because Jesus' willed it or would it obey its natural circumstances? Which was more powerful to it: The desire of Jesus or the seasons?

Through Jesus our world was created (Colossians 1.15-16). The creator is always more powerful than the created. When we receive a promise from God, not even the natural circumstances which God created can prevent it from coming to pass. All we need is one thing: FAITH!

"As they passed by in the morning, they saw the fig tree withered away to its roots. And Peter remembered and said to him, 'Rabbi, look! The fig tree that you cursed has withered.' And Jesus answered them, 'Have faith in God. Truly, I say to you, whoever says to this mountain, "Be taken up and thrown into the sea," and does not doubt in his heart, but believes that what he says will come to pass, it will be done for him'" (Mark 11.20-23 ESV).

So when we are confronted with a choice between God's Promise and our natural circumstances (wind, giants and the seasons), we must ALWAYS put our faith in God's Promises. His Word usurps everything if we just believe.

"For we live by faith, not by sight" (2 Corinthians 5.7 NIV).

Sadly, if we put our faith into sight more than our faith, God's promises to us will wither and die. We can't bear supernatural fruit if we don't have faith. But, thankfully, God is a God of second chances. He will give us access to our Promised Land again and again until our faith in Him is bigger than our faith in our circumstances. Even, like the Israelites, if it takes us forty years to enter our Promised Land.

What natural circumstances are telling you that God's Promises are impossible or dead? Today, will you put your faith in God's Word and not let doubt attack your belief? If you haven't received a promise from the Lord, will you seek Him and His will for your life? Put all your faith in God's Promises, trusting that He is more powerful than the situation you face.

"Jesus looked at them and said, 'With man this is impossible, but with God all things are possible'" (Matthew 19.26 NIV).

Thin Air

My husband loves jets. Ever since I met him when we were 16 years old, he has wanted to be a jet pilot. I watched through the years as God closed the doors to him joining the military while opening the doors for him to study medicine. Today, my husband is an ER doctor who still loves to watch jets fly.

One day, my husband was watching yet another YouTube video of a military pilot maneuvering a jet. He felt the Holy Spirit tell him to watch closely as the jet pilot gained speed and altitude. For the first several seconds, the jet steadily increased speed as it rocketed to the heavens. Towards the end of its climb, the jet began to gain speed faster and faster, and it began to go higher and higher more rapidly.

As the jet entered the thin air thousands of feet into the sky, the resistance holding the jet back loosened. The last few seconds of its ascent toward the zenith of its flight, the jet gained altitude and speed at almost supernatural rates. My husband felt the Holy Spirit compare the jet's flight to a Christian's walk of faith.

The closer our minds and hearts are toward the earth, there is much drag holding us back. We will gain speed and altitude in God's will slowly and with struggle. But the closer our minds and hearts are to heaven and to God's plan, the resistance loosens, and we are free to go at supernatural rates with God as our focus.

"Set your minds on things that are above, not on things that are on earth" (Colossians 3.2 ESV).

As Christians, there is much of our lives that will look like everyone else. We must eat, go to work, do our laundry, pay our bills and care for our families just like everyone else. However, our lives should pattern after the Bible and God's plan rather than the world's way of doing things. Where the world and God diverge, we should see a marked difference in our lives. There can be an excellence in all we do and a joy that is not dependent on our circumstances. If our gaze is on our Heavenly Father, much of our beliefs, thoughts, decisions and actions will be vastly different from the world.

"Do not conform to the pattern of this world, but be transformed by the renewing of your mind. Then you will be able to test and approve what God's will is—his good, pleasing and perfect will" (Romans 12.2 NIV).

These unique, heavenly patterns that we gain are what loosen us from the trappings of this world and rocket us into the thin air with God. When we finally let go of what the world deems as "normal," we will gain speed and altitude in our God-given destiny much more quickly and effectively. And though it may feel like we are the only ones living for God on earth, there is a "crowd of witnesses" watching us and rooting for us. Jesus is at the right hand of the Father, and they and the angels are all cheering us to the finish line. So let us let go of "every weight that slows us down," so we can soar into God's Kingdom, finishing the race that God has prepared for us (Hebrews 12.1).

"Who then will condemn us? No one—for Christ Jesus died for us and was raised to life for us, and he is sitting in the place of honor at God's right hand, pleading for us" (Romans 8.34 NLT).

Armor and Sword

"Put on all of God's armor so that you will be able to stand firm against all strategies of the devil. For we are not fighting against flesh-and-blood enemies, but against evil rulers and authorities of the unseen world, against mighty powers in this dark world, and against evil spirits in the heavenly places" (Ephesians 6.11-12 NLT).

My family and I spent our winter break in Colorado for some snow skiing in the Rocky Mountains. Being from South Texas where it almost never snows, getting ready for skiing was a laborious undertaking. We layered our clothes from long johns to snow pants and from sweaters to ski coats. Then we added all of the winter accessories: balaclavas, scarves, gloves, hats, boots, etc. And at this point, we still had all of our ski gear to manage: skis, poles, goggles and helmets. By the time we were ready to ski, we were unrecognizable under all of our gear!

As I got ready for our second day of skiing, I realized that almost all of the gear we were putting on our bodies were for protection from the cold and injury. Only the skis and poles truly enabled us to glide down the mountain.

Preparing for the slopes reminded me of the Amor of God. All but one piece of armor listed in Ephesians 6.10-17 is used for protection. Only the sword is an offensive tool. The rest of the armor is used defensively, protecting us from the environment and attackers. I wonder how many Christians go into battle wielding the sword without one stitch of armor on. It would be like skiing down the mountain without a helmet, jacket, goggles, snow pants or gloves. A person wouldn't last long in the treacherous conditions of the mountainscape, yet Christians go into spiritual battle naked and exposed against an enemy that feeds on their vulnerability.

I believe that before we can truly be decisive with the Sword of the Spirit, God's Holy Word the Bible, we must learn to protect ourselves from the ugly elements of spiritual warfare. It may seem cumbersome at first, verbally claiming and employing each piece of armor every day, but the sacrifice will be well worth it once we see how much longer we can last on the slopes of life. We can meditate on what it means to be armored from God, so we can be ready when the spiritual attack arises. Only when we are fully protected with our defensive armor should we engage in a battle with our offensive swords.

<u>Defensive Gear</u>

1) We can put on the Belt of Truth: "Stand your ground, putting on the belt of truth and the body armor of God's righteousness" (v 14).

Do we have any hidden secrets or motives? Are we walking in the Truth of God's Word, exposed completely to His care and direction? Are there any dark areas in our lives that the enemy can feed on and control? Do we have the Inspired Scriptures and God's promises fastened tightly to our lives, so we can distinguish the lies of Satan from God's Word? We can stand firmly on God's truth, trusting that our victory is achieved by our submission to God's Word and Will.

2) We can put on the Gospel Shoes of Peace: "For shoes, put on the peace that comes from the Good News so that you will be fully prepared" (v 15).

Are we ready to share the Good News of Jesus Christ when the opportunity presents itself? Do we have peace in our inner lives and the lives of our homes and family? It is very difficult to shine the Light of Christ to an external world if we are distracted by our hurts, pains and bitterness in our inner world. We must learn to forgive quickly and give our hurts to God right away, so the enemy can't fester in our wounds. We must fit our feet with the Shoes of Peace, so we journey with God on the destiny He has placed before us.

3) We can put on the Shield of Faith: "In addition to all of these, hold up the shield of faith to stop the fiery arrows of the devil" (v 16).

Do we have more faith in God's Word and His promises than we do in the circumstances surrounding us? Do the waves and winds of hardship cause us to lose our focus on Christ or is our gaze steadfast on the Cross? The enemy knows how to throw darts of doubt and fear at us, but we must guard our calling and destiny at all costs by holding our steadfast faith in front of us like a great shield. Our faith in God's Word and His promises will protect us from falling prey to hopelessness, bitterness, and sin. The enemy wants nothing more than to throw us off course, but our faith will pave the way for us to run the race to win.

4) We can put on the Helmet of Salvation: "Put on salvation as your helmet…" (v 17a).

Do we fully comprehend and claim the Finished Work of Jesus on the Cross and the Salvation we have received through the Blood of Jesus Christ? We have been made right with God and our sins have been forgiven because Jesus took our sins, died with them and rose again, leaving all of our ugliness behind. We receive new mercies every day, and we have God's power and favor that not only saves us from hell, but empowers us to live abundant and significant lives. Only when our salvation in Christ becomes bigger than our sins of humanity will we be protected from the lies and deceptions of the enemy.

Offensive Gear

5) Finally, we can grab hold of the Sword of the Spirit: "…and take the sword of the Spirit, which is the word of God (v 17b).

How do we use our Swords? We consume God's Words and wield His Truth found in the pages of the Bible. Using our own words that are rooted in belief, we can change the landscape around us by praying, interceding, teaching, encouraging, ministering, preaching, admonishing, prophesying, evangelizing, discipling, discerning, healing, giving, exhorting, etc. The more Scripture we consume, the sharper and more accurate our swords will be. We must learn, receive and believe God's Word, so we can use our faith-filled words to destroy the evil schemes of the enemy on earth. Our swords can do nothing unless we apply and activate God's Truth.

"Pray in the Spirit at all times and on every occasion. Stay alert and be persistent in your prayers for all believers everywhere" (v 18).

There is no coincidence that there are five articles in the Armor of God. The number 5 represents God's Goodness and Grace to humankind. This armor is a gift from God, and He gives us the grace we need to use this supernatural gear to achieve a life that has purpose and power. So let us no longer run into battle naked and exposed, wondering why we become easy targets for the enemy. Let us put on every piece of armor available to us, so we can wield our swords with confidence and accuracy!

David's Ragamuffins

"David left Gath and escaped to the cave of Adullam. When his brothers and his father's household heard about it, they went down to him there. All those who were in distress or in debt or discontented gathered around him, and he became their commander. About four hundred men were with him" (1 Samuel 22.1-2 NIV).

There are "D" words that have a negative stigma, but God is fully capable of turning them around. They are Distress, in Debt and Discontented.

The three "D" words caused men in the Old Testament to be unhappy in their current situation, so they risked it all and made their way to David. David was not yet king. In fact, David was a fugitive, running away from the current king who was trying to kill him. But as David learned to lean on the Lord, his men were exposed to what it means to be fully submitted to God.

And what happened with this complete abandonment to the Father was amazing. David and his men became renown across the land. They achieved victories that seemed almost supernatural with the help of their God who defended them. Because they have nothing else to lose, they committed themselves fully to the promise of

God in David's life. They overcame every obstacle, and their strength, cunning and bravery established a legacy in a new kingdom.

What promise did David cling onto as he hid in the caves, writing and singing songs on the harp to His God? David would soon be the King over all of Israel and a man after God's own heart. As these ragamuffins turned warriors gave themselves fully to David, they each became an integral part of his growing military force. Their names and deeds are written in the Bible for all generations to read and envision.

If we are carrying around one or all of these "D" words, we can throw ourselves to the mercy of God. He loves us, and He can do amazing things in us if we are submitted to Him. In fact, it is when we have nothing left to lose that we learn to be wholly submitted to the Lord. Sometimes being a ragamuffin is the best thing that could ever happen to us. God can turn our "D" words into words of victory, renown and strength.

"Now these are the chiefs of David's mighty men, who strongly supported him in his kingdom, together with all Israel, to make him king, in accordance with the word of the Lord concerning Israel" (1 Chronicles 11.10 AMP).

Weeping Wounds

"Any person with a serious skin disease must wear torn clothes, leave his hair loose and unbrushed, cover his upper lip, and cry out, 'Unclean! Unclean!' As long as anyone has the sores, that one continues to be ritually unclean. That person must live alone; he or she must live outside the camp" (Leviticus 13.45-56 MSG).

In the Old Testament, open sores on the body caused a person to be separated from the community. If he or she had weeping wounds, they would be considered outcasts until the wounds healed. If the wounds continued to ooze, this was a sign that infection had set in or the wound was not healing properly.

The ooze is the body's defense mechanism to clean the wound before the scab forms. There are two main reason why a wound keeps weeping. First, if the hurt person continually rips off the scab, the wound will reopen and continue to weep. Second, if infection has set into the wound, the body will continue to produce the ooze. This can occur if the wound is not cleaned and bandaged quickly and properly.

The Old Testament may seem harsh, but God was protecting His people during a time where science and medicine were limited. However, much of the physical applications of God's Word can be applied spiritually.

For example, there are many people today with emotional wounds that haven't been healed. They either keep reopening the wound, rehearsing and harboring their hurts for years and never allowing themselves to heal. Or they have not fully dealt with the hurt, and bitterness, anger and resentment have set in like an infection.

So many people have weeping wounds, and they don't realize that the ooze pouring from their sores is affecting every single relationship that they have.

"From the sole of your foot to the top of your head there is no soundness—only wounds and welts and open sores, not cleansed or bandaged or soothed with olive oil" (Isaiah 1.6 NIV).

The Bible says that we are like sandpaper to each other. In our normal interactions with people every day, we are going to bump and rub up against each other. This is a good thing, which will sharpen us and make us into the image of Christ. However, people who have multiple open emotional wounds that haven't healed will feel pain like knives penetrating their flesh every time someone rubs or bumps up against them in normal, everyday interactions.

"Iron sharpens iron, and one man sharpens another" (Proverbs 27.17 ESV).

These people cannot keep relationships well because their emotional wounds are disturbing their everyday life. They will eventually ostracize themselves from the communities around them because they can't heal properly, let alone be sharpened. Their marriages, families, jobs, ministries, etc., are all affected by wounds that haven't healed. The scary part is that weeping wounds can become part of someone's natural reality. Peace, victory and prosperity have now been replaced by fear, defeat and destitution—and this is not God's will for us!

"The thief's purpose is to steal and kill and destroy. My purpose is to give them a rich and satisfying life" (John 10.10 NLT).

The thing to remember is that yes, this life is not fair. Yes, we all receive wounds along the way, but the best thing we can do is allow God to heal them right away. We must let the Living Water of God's Spirit pour over our sores. Cleansing wounds can hurt and seeking help is humbling; but whether the wound was inflicted by others or by our own choices, we must let God clean it. Then, we need to allow God to bind up our wounds with His protection and care.

The bandage may mark us as broken, but by faith we know that healing is on the way! God promises in His Word that He can and will heal us. Job, one of the most wounded people that ever lived (both physically and emotionally) found healing with a deeper revelation of God. We can dig into God's Word and His rest in His presence, trusting that eventually we'll be able to do life with others without feeling pain with every rub and bump.

"For he wounds, but he also binds up; he injures, but his hands also heal" (Job 5.18 NIV).

Once Job humbled himself and allowed himself to be completely vulnerable to God, God was able to not only heal and restore him, but God blessed Job with greater abundance in his life. So take account of your life today. Do you struggle with relationships? Do you get offended and wounded easily? Do you have hurts from your past that you haven't been dealt with?

Even if you haven't acknowledged your sores yet, the weeping wounds you carry are oozing all over your relationships and life. Let God clean and bind your wounds today, so you can heal and get back into the community that God has called you to nurture and transform!

"So the Lord blessed Job in the second half of his life even more than in the beginning. For now he had 14,000 sheep, 6,000 camels, 1,000 teams of oxen, and 1,000 female donkeys. He also gave Job seven more sons and three more daughters" (Job 42.12-13 NLT).

Life Verse

I think we as parents have become so fearful of over-directing our kids that we have let go of our influence altogether. The Bible tells us that children are like arrows for us to influence, direct and guide into the image that God created them to be. We may never be perfect parents, but God has called us to be good stewards of the Ministry of Parenthood.

"Like arrows in the hands of a warrior are children born in one's youth" (Psalms 127.4 NIV).

"For we are God's handiwork, created in Christ Jesus to do good works, which God prepared in advance for us to do" (Ephesians 2.10 NIV).

An essential role of parenthood is being a seeker of what God says about our kids. An easy way to do this is to ask the Holy Spirit to give us at least one verse for each of them. The Bible contains God's promises that are all potentially ours if we learn to find, claim and apply them by faith. There is nothing wrong with we as parents seeking out God's promises and declaring them over our children. In fact, it should be encouraged as a tool that enables us to give our kids a sense of who they are in Christ! We can take time to pray and seek out those promises that the Holy Spirit wants to highlight for each soul we have been entrusted to nurture and guide.

My first-born son is now 12 years old. His name is Isaac Jeremiah. He is a child of promise, and he loves to make people laugh. The name Isaac embodies both of those attributes. But his life verse comes from his middle name, Jeremiah. I had been seeking a verse for him and one in particular kept coming to mind. When a friend sent me that verse in a text about my son, I knew this was his life verse.

"When I discovered your words, I devoured them. They are my joy and my heart's delight, for I bear your name, O Lord God of Heaven's Armies. I never joined the people in their merry feasts. I sat alone because your hand was on me. I was filled with indignation at their sins" (Jeremiah 15.16-17 NLT).

If you know my first-born, you would see how much he embodies this verse. He loves the Lord and His Word. And he very good at discerning right from wrong to the point that he many times does not fit in with the world around him. I call him my prophet.

My second born son is now 10 years old. His name is Levi Daniel. Levi means "joined," "attached," "connected" and "harmony." My middle child is like the glue between his two other siblings. He likes to keep the peace and he empathizes with both his older brother and younger sister. The Levites in the Bible were priests, but they also did many other things for the temple, like cooking, cleaning, carpentry, music, etc. I see music as part of his design and future.

"And you will know that I have sent you this warning so that my covenant with Levi may continue," says the Lord Almighty. "My covenant was with him, a covenant of life and peace, and I gave them to him; this called for reverence and he revered me and stood in awe of my name. True instruction was in his mouth and nothing false was found on his lips. He walked with me in peace and uprightness, and turned many from sin" (Malachi 2.4-6 NIV).

My second-born creates peace wherever he goes. He puts the feelings and concerns of others before his own, and he reveres the Lord and leads by example. I call him my shepherd.

My third-born child is my sweet 8-year-old girl. I so wanted to have a daughter, and I'm overjoyed that she is the baby of the family. Her name is Karis Ruth. Karis comes from the Greek word Charisse, which means "God's grace" with undertones of kindness and beauty. Ruth means "friendship" or "companion," so her two names together mean "a friend of grace." When I first received her verse, I wasn't sure I liked it. But when God explained it to me, I realized how important it was for her to know this promise and claim it.

"You are altogether beautiful, my darling; there is no flaw in you" (Song of Solomon 4.7 NIV).

We live in a society where the beauty of a woman is scrutinized in every way. The Song of Solomon is like a love letter from Jesus to His bride. We are the Bride of Christ, and because of Jesus' Finished Work on the Cross, we are flawless in the eyes of God. Regardless of how the world tries to define and categorize her, I want my daughter to know that she is beautiful and perfect through the Blood of Jesus, and her Heavenly Father adores and loves her. I call her my graceful companion.

So what about the souls in your life whom God has given you the ability to guide and influence? What Bible Verses can you claim and profess over them? All of God's Promises are theirs by faith, but we can choose tailor-made ones that suit their personality, design and purpose. So don't be shy about choosing Scripture for your children. Find lots of them and apply them liberally to the lives and hearts of your kids!

"For no matter how many promises God has made, they are 'Yes' in Christ. And so through him the 'Amen' is spoken by us to the glory of God" (2 Corinthians 1.20 NIV).

Lost Gold Ring

I recently lost a gold ring that my husband picked out and surprised me with several years ago. We were in Colorado for a family ski trip, and my ring size dropped about a quarter size because of the cold. The ring must have slipped off my finger during the day as I put on and took off my gloves.

We called different stores and retraced our steps, but I had a feeling that God was using my ring for His purposes. Usually, I'll put my faith into God's will to bless and prosper us, but on this occasion, I felt God call me to make a sacrifice. My ring was needed for a bigger purpose.

I sense there was a young lady in need. She was a college student in financial straits and my ring was just what she needed to know that God was looking out for her. I finally gave up looking for my ring and started praying for the vision of this young lady that God had given me instead. I prayed specifically that my ring would remind her that there is a God who is watching out for her and who loves her.

A week later, I lost another ring. This ring was a silver ring with my daughter's birthstone on it. I was so frustrated and angry with myself. I'm usually a very good steward of my possessions. I have a keen awareness that I must be responsible for what I have or else God will not entrust me with more, and this truth encompasses more than just property. It includes things like jobs, relationships, influence, time, etc.

I looked all over my house and thought about where I might have left my ring, but I came up empty-handed. I prayed again to God, expressing my frustration and wondering what He would tell me.

I felt Him say, "Alisa, the other ring I asked you to give up, but this ring is yours. Do you believe that I can find it for you?"

Although I had looked everywhere, I chose to put my faith in God's will to find my ring. "Yes, God, I know You can lead me to that ring." I instantly stopped fretting about it. God said He would find it for me, and I believed Him at His Word. I went back to my computer to finish some writing.

As I began writing, I felt like I needed to look at my wedding ring. I lifted my hand, and instead of seeing two rings (my engagement ring and wedding band), I saw three rings on my ring finger. The ring with my daughter's birthstone was sandwiched between my engagement ring and wedding band. Without realizing it, I had put all three rings on that morning.

I was overjoyed that my ring was found, but I knew God was teaching me something. I opened my heart to Him, and I felt Him say, "I am fully capable of finding anything you lose. But sometimes, I want to use your blessings to bless others. Just because you feel like you have lost something, doesn't mean that I have lost it. I will continue to use what you lose for My Kingdom and eternal purposes."

I realized that this life is full of loss. We may lose relationships, jobs, influence and things; but nothing is lost to God. He can bring those things back to us by faith or He will use those things in the lives of others. We simply need to trust that even though the blessing is no longer a part of our lives, God is still using all things for His glory and to bless His Children. We can trust God with everything.

"If you cling to your life, you will lose it; but if you give up your life for me, you will find it" (Matthew 10.39 NLT).

American Girl Dream

I went to New York City several years ago with two of my friends. As we walked down the city streets, we passed the American Girl Store. I had to stop in and look around. Although my daughter was not even two years old at the time, I couldn't wait to jump into the world of the American Girl. I love the entire theme of the dolls, the books, the movies, the crafts, the variety, and I couldn't help but be swept up in my childish imagination.

I brought the doll home and surprised my daughter for her second birthday. Needless to say, she only saw a doll—not an American Girl Doll from New York City! She never played with her, and the poor thing got neglected. My daughter even grew a bit fearful of her doll a few years later. Every time I would see the doll just lying in my daughter's closet, I felt sad that my American Girl dream would never be realized.

Now let's flash forward six years. My twin sister's daughter is only two weeks younger than my little girl. And they are both turning eight years old. She decided to buy her daughter an American Girl Doll for her birthday. I talked with my husband, and we agreed to give the American Girl dream one more try. We ordered my daughter a new doll to see if this would transform her fear into joy.

When my daughter opened her present, she was so excited. She loved the doll! She even found her old American Girl, brushed her hair and changed her clothes. Now she has two dolls that she plays with and adores. I happened to glance on the box of the American Girl, and sure enough, the box read, "Dolls for 8 plus." I had almost ruined the entire American Girl experience for my daughter because I was not patient. I should have simply laid my desires aside and waited for the right time instead of pushing my agenda.

Just a few days ago, we went to the store and bought a few American Girl books, and my daughter has been ravishingly reading them. Now she has two dolls, a pet, the crafts and the books—all American Girl. I'm so excited to be head-first into American Girl nation! This lesson highlighted a truth that God has been revealing to me.

God knows the desires of our hearts, but He will not unleash them until He sees the time is right and we are ready. I look back to all my years of waiting for God's promises, and I'm so grateful that God shut many doors. I remember feeling like God let me down, but it was my own expectations that let me down. God always does what is right for us, and He can transform our heartache into powerful victories when we trust Him. If we get our promises too early, we might not appreciate them. We may even fear them! So it's best to wait on God, cling onto faith and trust that God will fulfill every single promise He has given us according to His timetable.

"The Lord isn't really being slow about his promise, as some people think. No, he is being patient for your sake. He does not want anyone to be destroyed, but wants everyone to repent" (2 Peter 3.9 NLT).

"I wait for the Lord, I expectantly wait, and in His word do I hope" (Psalm 130.5 AMP).

Tapestry of Thorns

The opposite of worry is peace. If our thoughts make a blanket for our minds, worry would create a tapestry of thorns and peace would create a fleece of comfort. Which one sounds more pleasing for us to curl up in?

Our brains consist of the most unique, specialized tissue in the body. Its condition and health effects every aspect of our being—mind, body and soul. Wrapping our brains with a tapestry of worry will elevate a negative environment in our lives, which can lead to damaging effects. This is why the Bible expressly commands us to take captive every thought.

"We destroy arguments and every lofty opinion raised against the knowledge of God, and take every thought captive to obey Christ" (2 Corinthians 10.5 ESV).

We wouldn't wrap a baby in tapestry of thorns, yet we do this daily with the delicate and precious tissues of our mind. Jesus promises us that we can have peace. This peace doesn't always come intuitively or from our current circumstances. This peace is a gift from Jesus Christ, but we must receive His peace like a soft, fleece blanket and put it around us.

"Peace I leave with you; my peace I give you. I do not give to you as the world gives. Do not let your hearts be troubled and do not be afraid" (John 14.27 NIV).

Jesus says He is giving us His peace, but we must accept it, take off the tapestry of thorns and wrap our lives in it. The enemy wants us to live in worry, doubt and defeat, and He is constantly accusing us before God (Revelation 12.10). However, Jesus is always interceding on our behalf at the right hand of the Father (Romans 8.34). Every moment we have two blankets being offered to us—the worry of the enemy or the peace of Jesus.

Jesus desires to fill our lives with joy, strength, prosperity and victory; but we must start with claiming His peace. There will always be a blanket wrapping our minds, but we can choose daily which blanket we want. Do we want the scraping thorns of the enemy or the gentle fleece of Jesus Christ?

"Do not be anxious about anything, but in every situation, by prayer and petition, with thanksgiving, present your requests to God. And the peace of God, which transcends all understanding, will guard your hearts and your minds in Christ Jesus" (Philippians 4.6-7 NIV).

So choose peace today and let the worry fall by the wayside. Worry doesn't add a single day to your life; in fact, it will only rob you of the minutes you waste doing it!

"And which of you by being anxious can add a single hour to his span of life?" (Matthew 6.27 ESV).

"Hope deferred makes the heart sick, but a longing fulfilled is a tree of life" (Proverbs 13.12 NIV).

The Bible affirms that we will have to wait for God's promises to be fulfilled, especially the promises in which our hearts are tightly woven. We may often wonder why God seems to postpone our promises for a while, but the answer is simple. He doesn't just want to give us one fruit of blessing. He wants to give us a "Tree of Life" with many fruits of blessing.

God loves us so much that a single blessing isn't good enough. He desires to make our lives into a factory of blessings. Sometimes we get caught up in a single promise of God that we can't comprehend God's greater vision of what He's accomplishing. He will use us as portals of blessings if we are patient in His movements and timing.

The Bible says that God will turn the curse of our waiting, our emptiness, our stigma, our lack, our longing, etc., and make us into a source of blessing to others. This truth should make us strong in our waiting. We don't have to be afraid that God will not fulfill His promises. Although our hearts may ache while we wait, we can trust that God is producing greatness in our patience.

"Among the other nations, Judah and Israel became symbols of a cursed nation. But no longer! Now I will rescue you and make you both a symbol and a source of blessing. So don't be afraid. Be strong, and get on with rebuilding the Temple!" (Zechariah 8.13 NLT).

The Tree of Life is in fact Jesus Christ Who is the source of every blessing. Why would we simply want the blessing when we can have the Blessing Maker? God's growing the Tree of Life in the center of our lives, so He can cultivate a harvest of His goodness in us, allowing the world to be benefactors of the fruit.

"Whatever is good and perfect comes down to us from God our Father, who created all the lights in the heavens. He never changes or casts a shifting shadow" (James 1.17 NIV).

Saint Patrick

"You intended to harm me, but God intended it for good to accomplish what is now being done, the saving of many lives" (Genesis 50.20 NIV).

Saint Patrick was not Irish, but he is now known as the patron saint of Ireland. How did this young English man make such an influence in Ireland during the 4th century AD? God was able to use what was meant for harm to spread the Gospel of Jesus Christ.

Saint Patrick's real name is believed to have been Maewyn Succat, and he was kidnapped at the age of 16 and sold into slavery in Ireland for about 6 years. He watched over his master's cattle until one day God told him that there was a ship waiting for him. He finally made his way back home and dedicated his life to God.

He spent the next decade studying under his mentor, St. Germain, the bishop of Auxerre. One night he had a dream that the people of Ireland were calling out to him. He received the Pope's blessing to return to the very people who enslaved him, and he began a massive spiritual awakening in the hearts of the pagan people.

He became a Christian missionary and first bishop to Ireland. Not only did he win many souls to Christ (including both the rich and the poor), he established monasteries, schools and churches all over Ireland.

Because of Saint Patrick's time as a slave in Ireland, he knew the language and culture of the Irish people, and he could preach to them in a way that they could understand. He had so much zeal for the Lord that even after being arrested many times by the Celtic Druids, he still continued his quest to win the hearts of the Irish People with the Good News of Jesus Christ.

Although many legends have been added to this special holiday, Saint Patrick's Day began with an evil done to a young man that God turned into good.

We live in an imperfect world, and God sometimes allows bad things to happen to His children, but we must always remember that God is fully capable of turning what was meant for evil into something meant for our good.

"And we know that in all things God works for the good of those who love him, who have been called according to his purpose" (Romans 8.28 NIV).

The Bible is filled with stories of God transforming horrible situations into triumphant testimonies.

When we trust God and stay obedient to the fruition of His plan, we will get a front-row seat to how He supernaturally transforms our pains and hurts into our biggest victories. God will make us into a blessing via the curses we've been given if we simply trust and obey Him.

"Just as you, Judah and Israel, have been a curse among the nations, so I will save you, and you will be a blessing. Do not be afraid, but let your hands be strong" (Zechariah 8.13 NIV).

Cake of Life

My daughter and I love to bake together. She doesn't especially love cooking healthy meal recipes with me, but if I'm creating a dessert, she has her apron on and mixing spoon ready. On this particular afternoon, we were making two lemon pound cakes. One for my family and one for my ladies' church small group that I lead.

The process of this pound cake was somewhat complex, and since we doubled the ingredients, we had a lot of batter we were working with. My daughter sifted the dry ingredients as I scooped them into the sifter—flour, salt and baking soda. And in another bowl, we creamed together two pounds of butter, 6 cups of sugar, a dozen eggs and a few splashes of vanilla.

Once we were done with our two bowls of mix, we had to combine them into a single bowl. We added parts of the dry ingredients to the wet ingredients while incorporating two cups of sour cream one spoonful at a time. As we started adding and mixing, I began to realize that the bowl was almost too small to hold all the ingredients. I had to be very careful to use the beater slowly, so the dry ingredients wouldn't fly out of the bowl. I thought about all the work we had completed before this point, and I didn't want to mess up the batter at the end. We had put too much effort into these cakes to ruin them in the last stages of their creation.

As I was methodically and carefully beating the batter, the Bible verse from Ezekiel about how it's better to be a wicked person who turns away from sin at the end of his life than to be a righteous person who becomes unfaithful at the end of his life came to mind. Of course, as Christians, we all have been saved by the Blood of Jesus alone, but there is a truth to be found in these verses for all of us.

"But if a wicked person turns away from all the sins they have committed and keeps all my decrees and does what is just and right, that person will surely live; they will not die. None of the offenses they have committed will be remembered against them. Because of the righteous things they have done, they will live…. But if a righteous person turns from their righteousness and commits sin and does the same detestable things the wicked person does, will they live? None of the righteous things that person has done will be remembered. Because of the unfaithfulness they are guilty of and because of the sins they have committed, they will die" (Ezekiel 18.21-24 NIV).

What I realized is that the fullness of our lives is like a cake—everything we choose to do each day adds ingredients and effort into the making of our life. If we mess up during the beginning of our lives with bad choices and action but turn our lives to Jesus, He in His infinite imagination can create something beautiful out of our mess. Our cake may not be the lemon pound cake that we started with, but God can use the ingredients around us to make it into something amazing if we give Him control. By the time our lives are complete, we will have a beautifully prepared cake for God's glory.

However, we can live all our lives for God from a young age, allowing Him to add ingredients and stir us in certain ways, and our cake can be well on its way to being great. But it doesn't matter what we accomplish on the way; if we walk away from God and our life of faith, the batter of what God is doing will not come to fruition. God can't continue to prepare us if we decide we don't want His help anymore. Just like my lemon pound cake—if I would have left it undone at the end, it doesn't matter how much ingredients and effort I added previously, my cake would not be complete.

That is why the Apostle Paul says we need to finish in faith, not just start in faith: "I have fought the good fight, I have finished my race, I have kept the faith" (2 Timothy 4.7 NIV).

We have a choice whether or not we will stay committed to what God is preparing in our lives. We can't simply live on the victories of yesterday. It would be so tempting to quit while we were ahead, and spend our lives pointing to what we accomplished in the past. But God has new mercies for us each day to achieve new victories.

"The faithful love of the Lord never ends! His mercies never cease. Great is his faithfulness; his mercies begin afresh each morning" (Lamentations 3.22-23 NLT).

God is preparing our lives like cakes, and there are more ingredients and processes He wants to add if we let Him. We can be patient with God and not become so proud of anyone victory that we feel like God has nothing more for us. Only until the timer dings for the cake to be done should we ever feel like we have finished our race.

"The end of a matter is better than its beginning, and patience is better than pride" (Ecclesiastes 7.8 NIV).

Hazy View

Sometimes you have to turn off the lights to get a better view...

Since the spring daylight saving, every morning I wake up and darkness still quietly lingers around the house. I turn on the lights in the living room and kitchen and begin to cook breakfast for my family. When I look out the back window from the kitchen, I can barely see the lights of cars passing down the neighborhood streets. The normal scene of my backyard— fences, the trees, the lake and other houses— are all shrouded in shadows.

"So we are lying if we say we have fellowship with God but go on living in spiritual darkness; we are not practicing the truth" (1 John 1.6 NLT).

One morning, I got up early, and as I walked into the kitchen, the window blinds were already open. I hadn't turned on any of the kitchen lights, so my eyes were able to focus on the illumination just outside my door. I could see street lights, car lights and house lights surrounding me, and I gained a clearer view of my backyard. Once I turned on the lights in the kitchen, however, the vision instantly vanished.

"The people who walk in darkness will see a great light. For those who live in a land of deep darkness, a light will shine" (Isaiah 9.2 NLT).

I turned off the lights again and gazed through the window once more. I was so impressed with how much I could perceive. I saw cars driving passengers to work, waterfowl taking in an early swim in the lake and the soft glow of stars in the distant, dark sky. I found it so amazing that I stood on the cusp of two worlds—the inside world and the outside world. When I turned on the kitchen lights, the outside world faded. When I turned off the kitchen lights, the outside world came alive.

"The light shines in the darkness, and the darkness has not overcome it" (John 1.5 NIV).

I thought of the spiritual applications of the light. As humans, we are beings of both spirit and flesh, and we stand on the cusp of two worlds: the spiritual and physical realms. Many times, God's movements seem shrouded in the shadows, and we feel like His direction for our lives is somehow lost in dark. But I wonder what would happen if we turned off the lights to our flesh and earthly security? Would our hazy view of eternity and God's plan become clearer?

"For he has rescued us from the dominion of darkness and brought us into the kingdom of the Son he loves" (Colossians 1.13 NIV).

Jesus is the great Light in the darkness. He is not hidden, and He is not invisible. Maybe the reason we can't see Him for a time is because He is walking the parameter of our lives, teaching us how to dim the inside lights of our flesh. He wants to expand our awareness of eternity, so He walks to farther corners of our view, so we can stretch and grow to see Him. We will always be people of two worlds until we reach heaven. Until then, if we are struggling to see Jesus, we may have to dim the lights of the physical world, so the spiritual world can become brighter in our sight.

"When Jesus spoke again to the people, he said, 'I am the light of the world. Whoever follows me will never walk in darkness, but will have the light of life'" (John 8.12 NIV).

Constant Victory

We have victory in Christ. As Christians, we enter into a paradigm shift from basing our worth on our own victories to basing our worth on Jesus' victory on the Cross.

"He gives us the victory through our Lord Jesus Christ" (1 Corinthians 15.57 NIV).

It seems strange and almost absurd to place our value on what someone else has done. Our culture may even look down on someone who walks in the victory of another. But we find freedom from human striving when we walk in the victory of the Cross because this victory is always constant.

"Jesus Christ is the same yesterday and today and forever" (Hebrews 13.8 NIV).

We learn early in our walk of faith that our failures do not define us, but to truly be free in the victory of the Cross, we can't let our triumphs define us either. Rather, we should live in a continuous state of victory through Jesus.

"No, despite all these things, overwhelming victory is ours through Christ, who loved us" (Romans 8.37 NLT).

God brings both victories and failures into our lives, but they are all part of His Ultimate Victory Plan. God can use closed doors and opened doors, weakness and strengths, trials and triumphs and sorrow and joy to accomplish His will on earth and in us.

"And we know that in all things God works for the good of those who love him, who have been called according to his purpose" (Romans 8.28 NIV).

Now since we are victorious in Christ, we can produce works that are rooted in that victory. We won't stop and stare at anyone victory because God's plan of "victory through our faith" continues until His Ultimate Victory Plan is complete.

"Loving God means keeping his commandments, and his commandments are not burdensome. For every child of God defeats this evil world, and we achieve this victory through our faith. And who can win this battle against the world? Only those who believe that Jesus is the Son of God" (1 John 5.3-5 NLT).

Promise Progression

Based on Acts 9.38-42 (NLT)

God uses Peter to perform a miracle: He brings Tabitha back to life! As I read these verses, I realized that they illustrate the process of God planting and awakening His promises in our lives. It may seem odd that our promises must die in the natural, but our faith will ignite a supernatural resurrection that will demonstrate the power and love of God through His Son, Jesus Christ!

- "But the believers had heard that Peter was nearby at Lydda, so they sent two men to beg him, 'Please come as soon as possible!'"

God sends godly people to encourage us in our promise and to guide us to our destination.

- "So Peter returned with them; and as soon as he arrived, they took him to the upstairs room. The room was filled with widows who were weeping and showing him the coats and other clothes Dorcas had made for them."

Our promises will always fill a need, mend broken hearts and bring people closer to Jesus, but we must recognize that the promise is not just for our own benefit. It should help the lost and hurting around us.

- "But Peter asked them all to leave the room; then he knelt and prayed. Turning to the body he said, 'Get up, Tabitha.'"

God will separate us from everyone until we are alone with our promise, and we will acknowledge that our promise is dead in the natural. But we can touch the dead promise by faith and wait for it to supernaturally respond to us.

- "And she opened her eyes! When she saw Peter, she sat up!"

The promise will react to the person it is destined for and be awaken in the supernatural. Our promises will rise up out of lack, drought and death.

- "He gave her his hand and helped her up."

Once the promise awakens, it is up to us to reach out and take hold of it by faith. The dead will come to life if we believe that God desires it.

- "Then he called in the widows and all the believers, and he presented her to them alive."

When God performs a miracle, the people closest to us will see it first and rejoice. God wants to bring our promises to life so others can see His movements in our lives.

- "The news spread through the whole town, and many believed in the Lord."

God uses our resurrected promises to spread the Good News of Jesus Christ to nonbelievers and to share His goodness and love with His Children.

Victory Made Easy

My son performs in the local youth orchestra. He practiced the piano for months, and it was finally his time to shine on stage. He performed beautifully along with his fellow musicians. They played in a large performance hall where the city orchestra holds their concerts. As I listened to the students play, I realized how hard they must have worked. Their two songs were long, so they each practiced for hours over many weeks.

Although they played well, it was obvious that they did not play as well as the professional musicians in the city orchestra. I have listened to this orchestra play classical and modern music, and they perform flawlessly. They play so well, that it is difficult to comprehend the years of practice and the thousands of hours they have poured into their chosen instrument. They make performing look so easy that an audience may overlook the effort, energy and time that it took to achieve their level of proficiency.

As I compared the youth orchestra to the professional orchestra, I wondered how many people look at Christians living in victory and take for granted all the effort, energy and time they devote to praying to God and reading, studying and obeying His Word. People may assume that these Christians are just lucky, but God says specifically in His Word that He leads us on paths of righteousness (Proverbs 2.20). That doesn't mean life will always be easy; but as we obey Him, He will give us everything we need each day to overcome all obstacles and accomplish His desired will (2 Peter 1.3).

As we witness Christians living in victory and see that their lives and home are filled with peace, joy and hope; we must assume that they are reading their Bibles, praying in the Spirit and obeying God's Word to the best of their ability. God is the source of everything that is good, and people who have lots of godly fruit in their lives are feeding on that goodness (Psalm 34.8 and Galatians 5.22-23). They are building their faith with the goodness of God, and their lives are set on righteous paths.

"For I am not ashamed of the gospel, because it is the power of God that brings salvation to everyone who believes: first to the Jew, then to the Gentile. For in the gospel the righteousness of God is revealed—a righteousness that is by faith from first to last, just as it is written: 'The righteous will live by faith'" (Romans 1.16-17 NIV).

But we shouldn't compare ourselves. Just as it will take the youth orchestra years of practice to enter the professional level, it will take us time to make the life of faith look easy. We can continue to seek and obey the Lord, and God will be pleased with our performance on each level of our journey with Him (2 Corinthians 2.15). And He will give us victory in every area of our lives if we just have faith that He always wants the best for us.

"For everyone born of God is victorious and overcomes the world; and this is the victory that has conquered and overcome the world—our [continuing, persistent] faith [in Jesus the Son of God]" (1 John 5.4 AMP).

The First Step

I tweeted this quote the other day. In my mind, I could see an entire process of repentance and redemption taking place in my life, but on Twitter I only have 140 characters or less to explain a Biblical Truth: Repentance leads to Redemption. The first and most important example of this truth is salvation.

"Therefore repent and return, so that your sins may be wiped away, in order that times of refreshing may come from the presence of the Lord" (Acts 3.19 NASB).

REPENT. RETURN. REFRESH.

When we realize that we are sinners and ask Jesus into our hearts, He's able to redeem our entire lives supernaturally and reconcile us back to God. If Jesus can redeem us from hell, He can certainly redeem us from the symptoms of hell—defeat, depression, poverty, bitterness, heartache, pain, etc.

We can now host "the presence of the Lord" on earth because we have righteousness through Jesus Christ, and we enjoy a "refreshing" relationship with the Holy Spirit. The process of redemption starts when God replaces our eternity separated from Him (hell) with eternity reconciled to Him (heaven).

"For you have been born again, not of perishable seed, but of imperishable, through the living and enduring word of God" (1 Peter 1.23 NIV).

But that's only the first step. The process of repent, return and refresh can be seen like a wellspring in our hearts. The Seed of Salvation springs to life when we receive salvation. It has supernaturally saved us, but now God wants to work that salvation into all the natural parts of our bodies, mind, hearts and lives. Every time we repent of sin, the Seed of Salvation can flow into more areas of our lives. The more we repent as the Holy Spirit convicts, the deeper and wider that wellspring spreads.

"For the kind of sorrow God wants us to experience leads us away from sin and results in salvation. There's no regret for that kind of sorrow. But worldly sorrow, which lacks repentance, results in spiritual death" (2 Corinthians 7.10 NLT).

If we feel defeated in a certain area, we may need to repent. Repentance is not bad at all. Repentance is learning to trade up. It's giving God something mediocre and requesting something better. It's confessing that we did it our way and the results weren't good, so we give up control and are ready to trust God's Best Plan.

God has a Kingdom Plan He is implementing on earth and in each of our lives. His Plan is for our peace, future and hope (Jeremiah 29.11), but we must let God have His way in our lives. As we repent of our stubborn will, He can move us further into His Kingdom Plan. Repentance will always be a huge part of a Spirit-filled person's life who is transforming the external world as her internal world is being transformed.

"From that time Jesus began to preach and to say, 'Repent, for the kingdom of heaven is at hand'" (Matthew 4.17 NKJV).

I recently took a Broadway trip to New York City. My little sister and I attended three Broadway shows, shopped all over the city and ate at lots of great restaurants. Everything went smoothly until the plane ride home. Since my sister lives in another state, I dropped her off at her gate before heading to mine. Her first flight was delayed and her second flight was canceled, but thankfully she got on standby and made it home in time for dinner.

My first flight was slightly delayed but otherwise went smoothly. It was my second of three flights that drastically hindered my course. There were tornadoes in Georgia and thunderstorms in North Carolina. We sat on the runway for almost three hours until the captain had to take us back to the gate. I entered the terminal and made my way to the longest line imaginable to rebook my next two flights.

As I stood in line, I got an email that my flights were rebooked for the following morning. I was so disappointed. I earnestly missed my kids and husband, and I looked forward to seeing them that day. I looked at the long line in front of me. I couldn't even see the help desk that it led to. Then I analyzed the arrival and departure board. It was littered with canceled and delayed flights. Finally, I opened the weather app on my phone. The forecast called for storms all day and into the night. Would my efforts to get an earlier flight even be worth it? That's when I thought to myself, "Perhaps the Lord will act on my behalf."

As I waited in line, I called the airline. Three attempts to connect with a customer service representative failed, but I wouldn't give up. Finally, I got a hold of them after an hour of standing in line with the phone to my ear. The customer service representative was able to book me two flights that would get me home by 11.30 that night. I was so excited! Since I was almost to the front of the line, I decided to confirm my seats and get my tickets printed.

When I got to the ticketing agent, he looked up the flights to my hometown. He said that there was an even earlier flight leaving in a few minutes, but it was almost done boarding. He quickly printed the tickets for me, and I ran to the gate. When I got on the plane, my seat was taken. The flight attendant said I would have to get off and talk with an agent. Luckily, an airline manager was at my gate, and he escorted me back on the plane and gave me the only seat left available.

Instead of getting home late at night, I got home at 8pm. I could see my kids! As I hugged each one of them, I thought about all the odds that were against me getting home early. If I would have just settled for the flights rebooked for the following day, I wouldn't be holding them at that moment. I knew that God had acted on my behalf because I took a chance. My luggage may be stuck on the morning flight, but I was already home.

Jonathan in the Bible also took a chance. He saw the army before him and said, "Perhaps the Lord will act in our behalf. Nothing can hinder the Lord from saving, whether by many or by few" (1 Samuel 14.6 NIV). Sometimes the odds against our situation are great, but that doesn't mean we shouldn't try. Instead of basing our decisions on our circumstances, we should base them on God. There is nothing too hard for God to do if He wills it.

Yes, God may close the door. He may have different plans that include delays, detours and destination changes. But our hearts and minds should be always aware that God is bigger than the long lines, cancellation boards and storms of life. He can achieve the impossible if we don't give up and keep moving forward. No situation is hopeless if we allow the word, "perhaps," to be at the forefront of our thoughts and trust that God is bigger than our situation.

"I am the LORD, the God of all mankind. Is anything too hard for me?" (Jeremiah 32.27 NIV).

Wine without Dregs

"Moab has been at rest from youth,
   like wine left on its dregs,
not poured from one jar to another—
   she has not gone into exile.
So she tastes as she did,
   and her aroma is unchanged."
- (Jeremiah 48.11 NIV).

Before we ask Jesus to be our Lord and Savior, we are like "wine left on its dregs," meaning we are filled with the sediments of sin.

"For everyone has sinned; we all fall short of God's glorious standard" (Romans 3.23 NLT).

The Bible says that if we accept Jesus into our hearts, we will be poured into a new jar, which purifies us and leaves behind the sediment of sin.

"If you declare with your mouth, 'Jesus is Lord,' and believe in your heart that God raised him from the dead, you will be saved" (Romans 10.9 NIV).

In order to be freed from sin, our old selves must die, so we can be resurrected to a new life that has been perfected by Jesus.

"We were therefore buried with him through baptism into death in order that, just as Christ was raised from the dead through the glory of the Father, we too may live a new life" (Romans 6.4 NIV).

Since our new selves are in Jesus, we are now "pure" and "holy" and "made right" in the eyes of God.

"God has united you with Christ Jesus. For our benefit God made him to be wisdom itself. Christ made us right with God; he made us pure and holy, and he freed us from sin" (1 Corinthians 1.30 NLT).

We can now have a relationship with God because the sin that separated us has been resolved.

"For Christ also suffered once for sins, the righteous for the unrighteous, to bring you to God. He was put to death in the body but made alive in the Spirit" (1 Peter 3.18 NIV).

When we accept Jesus into our lives, we become a new, perfected creation in Christ.

"This means that anyone who belongs to Christ has become a new person. The old life is gone; a new life has begun!" (2 Corinthians 5.17 NLT).

Since we are a new creation, the only way we can sin is if we believe and act on the lies of Satan who only wants to destroy our purified image in Christ.

"The thief comes only to steal and kill and destroy; I have come that they may have life, and have it to the full" (John 10.10 NIV).

Satan sees that we have been changed by the Blood of Jesus Christ, so his sole desire is to cause us to use our free will to behave like him. But thanks be to God, the Blood of Jesus continually cleanses us!

"But if we walk in the light, as he is in the light, we have fellowship with one another, and the blood of Jesus, his Son, purifies us from all sin" (1 John 1.7 NIV).

Don't let the enemy tempt you to forget who you are in Christ. You are a new creation that is blameless before God. Your old self has died, and your new self has been made right with God by the cross.

- You are holy and blameless: "Yet now he has reconciled you to himself through the death of Christ in his physical body. As a result, he has brought you into his own presence, and you are holy and blameless as you stand before him without a single fault" (Colossians 1.22 NLT).

- You are a royal priesthood: "But you are a chosen people, a royal priesthood, a holy nation, God's special possession, that you may declare the praises of him who called you out of darkness into his wonderful light" (1 Peter 2.9 NIV).

- You are victorious: "But thanks be to God! He gives us the victory through our Lord Jesus Christ" (1 Corinthians 15.57 NIV).

- You are co-heirs with Christ: "Now if we are children, then we are heirs—heirs of God and co-heirs with Christ, if indeed we share in his sufferings in order that we may also share in his glory" (Romans 8.17 NIV).

Jesus tucked you inside of His perfection, and proof of His Finished Work on the Cross is the indwelling of the Holy Spirit. We could not have God's Sprit in us if we were not made right in God's eyes.

"Don't you realize that all of you together are the temple of God and that the Spirit of God lives in you?" (1 Corinthians 3.16 NIV).

Gaining Territory

"The Lord gives the Word. And the women who tell the good news are many. The kings of armies run. They run away. And she who stays at home divides the riches. When you lie down among the sheep, you are like the wings of a dove covered with silver, and the end of its wings with shining gold. When the All-powerful divided the kings there, snow was falling in Zalmon" (Psalm 68.11-14 NLV).

There are thousands of promises in God's Word, the Bible, that are potentially ours when we learn how to find them, claim them and believe them by faith. God will give each one of us as many of those promises that we seek out and grasp. He also gives us promises in our spirits about our lives according to His best plans that He has for us. Finding Bible verses that affirm God's promises and speaking (or prophesying) those verses over ourselves will boost our faith and cast out all doubt.

We can start speaking God's Words over our lives instead of babbling our own imaginings, worries and fears. We can seek out God's promises and begin to claim them over and over again until they come to pass. We can write them down, take pictures of them, voice record them and say them any time doubt comes to rob our faith. Our faith is precious, and it gives God access to move supernaturally in our lives.

"The Lord gave the word; Great was the company of those who proclaim it: 'Kings of armies flee, they flee, And she who remains at home divides the spoil...'"

When we step out on God's promises, we begin to take ground that has not been claimed. The enemy doesn't like this and his cohorts are all over this desolate land. He doesn't want us to expand our territory because he knows we bring the Holy Spirit with us into our new property, furthering God's Kingdom on earth as it is in heaven (Matthew 6.10). We should expect hardships, setbacks and lots of waiting when we begin our march into God's promises.

But our main tactic of victory, besides perseverance, will be to use our words backed up by belief to profess our triumph. God wants us to win, but we must "remain" in His promises and never step back, relent or give up! We should always be taking new ground or holding our ground against attack. As Christians, we can come together and claim God's promises for others and for ourselves, like a host of brothers and sisters, staking out and establishing all the nations for Christ!

King David wrote Psalm 68, and he was aware of how difficult it was to take new ground for God. He also knew from experience that he needed to bring the Ark of the Covenant, which represents the Holy Spirit, into the land to have God's abundance and blessings (2 Samuel 6).

There are armies of the enemy that hate God, hate beauty, hate purity and hate good. God gives us grace and favor in order to overcome these oppressors, so we can be conduits of God's love and salvation to all people. God wants us to stretch out our borders, so we can bring the Holy Spirit into all the corners of the earth—pushing back the enemy into the abyss where he belongs (Revelation 20.3).

"The march of the good is opposed by enemies."
"The march of the good is marked by trials."*

We march into the wilderness of God's blessings; and as we use our words by faith, the deserts will transform into lush lands through the resurrection power of Jesus Christ. But we must first march into the wilderness, trusting that God will bring forth springs in the desert areas of our lives (Isaiah 41.18). The enemies will scatter and those who have waited and trusted on God will "divide the spoil" of God's blessings, favor and grace.

Christians can proclaim each victory, so that the lands of God's People expand across the earth. Walking into God's promises is not for the weak for faint of heart. We will have to stretch ourselves to the limits and fortify our faith. We will face giants and armies of evil kings, but greater is God who is in us than all the enemies of the world (1 John 4.4). When we rest in God's power and strength, no victory will be out of our reach!

"Though you lie down among the sheepfolds, You will be like the wings of a dove covered with silver, And her feathers with yellow gold."

Doing battle to claim new territory according to God's promises will be messy. In fact, David in this Psalm compares the fight to achieving God's promises to lying down in a sheepfold. The word sheepfold has two meanings. 1) It was the filthy holding pen for animals. 2) It was a tool used in the sacrifice of animals. When Jesus died for the sins of all mankind, the event was bloody and messy. He took the sins of the world and poured out His blood to cleanse all of us, so we could have a relationship with God—the ultimate victory!

This chaotic and messy event over 2,000 years ago released forgiveness, grace and favor across space and time. God promises us that though the fight will be messy, bloody and chaotic, we will be pure and clean like the wings of a dove, glowing gold and silver. God sees His goodness all over us because He sees us through the blood of Christ. We can't focus on the mess of the battle or else we will become discouraged and lose hope. Instead, we can focus on the ultimate victory that God has already won on our behalf!

"When the Almighty scattered kings in it, It was white as snow in Zalmon."

Finally, David makes a reference to a bloody battle of kings that took place on the mountain of Zalmon from Judges 9. This fight was messy. People plotted, attacked and murdered. The mountain of Zalmon was thick and dark with trees, and its history of fire and sin was just as thick and dark. But David prophesies over this mountain. He proclaims that God has scattered all the kings, the enemies of the Lord, and now the mountain is white as snow. This dense, dark mountain riddled with fires of schemers and haters is now covered in a blanket of moist, white snow—all evidence of the mess and chaos have been wiped clean!

If we can stay faithful to God, stepping out on His promises and not giving up when times get hard, He will supernaturally intervene. We will have the purity of doves and our Promised Land will gleam with God's presence.

*(The Preacher's Homiletic Commentary by Baker Books: Book 11 pg. 343-344).

Choice, not Force

"Then he took a cup, and when he had given thanks, he gave it to them, saying, 'Drink from it, all of you. This is my blood of the covenant, which is poured out for many for the forgiveness of sins'" (Matthew 26.27-28 NIV).

The first public miracle of Jesus was to turn water into wine at the Canaan Wedding. Jesus' mother saw lack in the celebration and knew only Jesus could provide. Jesus told the servants to pour more water into the six washbasins where the guests would rinse the grime of human effort off their hands (John 2.1-12). If water represents the Living Water of God or His Holy Spirit (Zechariah 14.8-9), we get this image of humans tainting God's pure water with our efforts—creating dirty water in the six basins.

But Jesus did not serve this dirty water to the wedding guests. He transformed the tainted water into the choicest Wine. Wine is symbolic of Jesus' Blood, which is Living Water rained down on the land, creating fruit that embodies water mixed with earth—wine instead of dirty water. Wine is like Jesus' Blood, God's Spirit made flesh or Immanuel, God with us. Wine is the New Covenant of Grace replacing the bitter vinegar of the Law, which was written by Moses for a people who thought they could meet God's Holy Standard on their own. Jesus' body was broken, pouring out this grace onto all of us, when we finally realized that we could not live up to God's holy standard on our own (Romans 3.23).

Jesus, born as a human baby, was destined to break His body for humankind, spilling His Redeeming Blood across space and time. Jesus is the Bread, broken to pour out His blood to reconcile all Six Days of Creation on the Seventh Day of Sabbath when God rested, knowing Jesus would finish the work of creation with reconciliation.

Jesus is Lord over the Sabbath, the Tree of Life planted in the earth next to the Tree of Knowledge, our free will to choose. God planted both trees in the Garden, ensuring that Jesus would reconcile the earth corrupted by our free will choices. Our free will came at the price of the Cross, and our human works are accepted by God through the Blood of Jesus.

God sent His Son, Jesus, to die, so we could have free will to love God by choice, not by force. Yes, we create sin when we disobey God's will, but God knew that we would also create free will gifts for His glory. God is the Creator and Owner of everything that exists. The only thing that we can give Him that He does not own is our free will to love and obey Him and create beauty for His glory.

God knew we would mess up with our free will, which is why He planted Jesus there with us when time began. God understood that we would—even in our messed-up human struggle—create thank offerings and free will offerings for Him. And our free will gifts done in our efforts washed in the Blood of the Lamb are beautiful, pleasing and acceptable in the eyes of God.

"Blessed are those who wash their robes, that they may have the right to the tree of life and may go through the gates into the city" (Revelation 22.14 NIV).

Heart Knowledge

I love when I read a book or listen to a sermon, and the speaker's words resonate in my heart. It's like my spirit rises up to the revelation being expressed, and the words encourage my faith. Somehow, my soul senses that truth from the Heart of God has been released, and my spirit captures the revelations hungrily.

I remember one such day. I heard an anointed prophet speak the Word of God, and her words were like spiritual nutrients to my soul. I was so encouraged by what she expressed that I tried to convey the information to my friends days later. But in my haste, I realized that I didn't have the right foundation to clearly express the ideas I had been given. My soaring faith had no concrete understanding from which to launch.

My problem was that the revelation was still in my heart, but I hadn't yet possessed it with my mind.

People many times talk about having head knowledge and no heart knowledge. This difficulty occurs when God's Word is in our mind, but it hasn't made its way to our heart yet. However, what I was suffering from was having heart knowledge without head knowledge. I knew the information that I had received was from God, but I couldn't explain it because I hadn't yet moved the words from my heart up to my head. God's revelation needs to be both places in order to make it our own.

We must have the heart knowledge and the head knowledge, so we can take ownership of the revelation and clearly articulate it. Our faith may be encouraged, but if we can't adequately explain the revelations to others, we won't be able to encourage the faith of the people around us. Similarly, if we have only religious knowledge without faith, people will not respond to our words no matter how learned we sound.

What I finally realized was that when my spirit leaps out to a specific revelation from a teacher, prophet, preacher or even a friend, I need to make that information my own. I've discovered that I must personally process the revelation knowledge, so I can effectively share what I've gleaned with others. Now before I share a revelation knowledge, I take time to dig into the Bible, ask the necessary questions and apply the truths to my life. I make the nugget of truth my own, so I can offer it to anyone that God brings in my path.

"Listen to the words of the wise; apply your heart to my instruction" (Proverbs 22.17 NLT).

"Getting wisdom is the wisest thing you can do! And whatever else you do, develop good judgment" (Proverbs 4.7 NLT).

Three Seagulls

"Hope deferred makes the heart sick, but a dream fulfilled is a tree of life" (Proverbs 13.12 NLT).

I remember many years ago, I went to the water's edge to pray about God's promises for my life. I had already waited so many years for my breakthrough, and I was discouraged and losing hope. As I was praying, I saw a great silver-colored fish floating in the water. He had died, and his scales flashed in the sun.

I knew soon the seagulls would come. Usually when food is thrown into the waves, many seagulls fly in to scoop up the pieces. But I believe this fish was so large that only the strongest seagulls gave it a chance.

The first seagull came from the north and hovered over the fish. Finally, He dipped down and grabbed the fish in his beak. He flapped his wings, but he could only bring the fish up several inches before letting it go. He turned away and flew back over the tops of the houses.

I waited. Less than a minute later another seagull came in from the east. He swooped down and captured the fish. The weight of the fish was heavy, and I could see his wings bend and pull against the load. He brought the fish up many feet before dropping it and flying away over the tops of the houses.

I waited. This time I almost gave up. I thought no seagull would be able to capture this fish. I felt the Holy Spirit tell me to look to the west. Coming in from the Laguna, I watched a large seagull fly in with a purpose. I had no doubt he was coming for the fish. His flight was straight and his decline was gradual.

When the great seagull reached the flashing silver in the water, he instantly grabbed the fish and his strong wings worked with the wind to pull it up with ease. He kept his prize secure and floated higher into the sky, soaring over the tops of houses.

The fish is symbolic of God's promise for me, and the first two seagulls are my attempts to pick it up in my own strength. God is allowing this process of trying and failing in my life to stretch my faith and make me more reliant on Him. I am learning to work with the Holy Spirit, and I'm growing stronger as I beat my wings in rhythm with His movements. I have peace knowing that someday I'll be that third seagull; and with God's strength, I'll carry the burden that comes with the blessing.

"But those who trust in the LORD will find new strength. They will soar high on wings like eagles. They will run and not grow weary. They will walk and not faint" (Isaiah 40.30-31 NLT).

Loopty-Loop Life

My daughter, the third child and last born of our family, leaned her back against the measuring stick. Her head was several centimeters into the green area of the line. I couldn't believe it. She could go on the rollercoaster ride. I could go on the rollercoaster ride!

We stepped into line, and my heart raced with excitement. This would be the first time I rode a rollercoaster ride complete with loopty-loops since my first child was born over twelve years ago.

The line went quickly, and several minutes later we stepped up to the closed gate as we watched the people in front of us board the rollercoaster seats. They strapped in, and I explained to my daughter about the seat belts and the overhead guard that would lock around us. Then I watched my sons standing with their dad in the line to the right of us. They would be sitting in front of us on the rollercoaster.

Here we were: a family of five about to experience something together that we have never done before. I used to watch other people get onto rides. With a baby at my hip and toddlers running around my feet, the days of independent movements seemed to be over.

But they weren't.

I stood with three kids that my husband and I had fed, changed, clothed and cared for over the years. And they stood tall and independent like olive shoots.

"Your wife will be like a fruitful vine within your house; your children will be like olive shoots around your table" (Psalm 128.3 NIV).

Olive shoots grow from the roots of the existing tree. These shoots will grow their own root systems, and after a time the shoots will need to be separated from the main tree and planted in their own section of land. The saplings then will be stripped of any leaves and fruit, so they can focus all their energy on strengthening their own secure root system.

Only when the saplings are strong on their own should we expect fruit from them.

The gate opened, and my family and I all got into our seats of the rollercoaster. Once we were all strapped in, I looked at my sweet olive shoots—not ready to be saplings, yet having root systems of their own.

I loved this new phase in our family. Every ride of life's rollercoaster that I missed while raising my three kids seemed small in comparison to the amazing "olive shoots around my table." Now here we were, riding one of life's rollercoaster rides together—each of us strapped into our own seat for the adventure.

I thanked God for that moment. I knew He was speaking to me. He showed me that although my kids couldn't fit on my hip anymore, they were each safe in His protective arms. And God was about to move my family into a new adventure in life—complete with loopty-loops!

"Start children off on the way they should go, and even when they are old they will not turn from it" (Proverbs 22.6 NIV).

A Promise

Why does God give us promises? If having a relationship with Him through Jesus Christ was His only agenda, why wouldn't He take us right to heaven after we receive salvation?

God's promises Mold us and Make us. They Mold us into the image of Christ and they Make us into coheirs with Him, claiming our inheritance on earth as it is in heaven (Matthew 6.10, Romans 8.17 and Ephesians 1.11).

We first receive His promises in our state of selfishness, but by the time those promises come to fruition, we have matured through the trials we faced in attaining them. God's promises are like tethers from us to the throne, drawing us closer in relationship with God. As we reach for these promises, God is able to transform us into His best image of us. But we can't let go or give up.

The theme of God's promises is all throughout the Bible. And we can get a glimpse of how these promises affect people by their reaction to them.

God's promises tear you to pieces: (Hosea 6.1).
God's promises rip out your heart: (Ezekiel 36.26).
God's promises build your faith: (Colossians 2.7).

God's promises give you a purpose: (Jeremiah 29.11).

God's promises mature your faith, mold you into the image of Christ, bring you closer to the throne of God and make you a servant to love. God's promises have nothing to do with self-promotion or self-glory and everything to do with loving God and others. They will bring you to your knees in prayer, desperation and repentance. And at one point in time, His promises will die in the natural, so they can be resurrected in the supernatural.

1. Naaman's promise of healing (2 Kings 5.1-19): He was a commander of a great army and had wealth, authority and prestige. He had done everything in his power to rid himself of leprosy. Desperate to be healed, he even listened to his wife's young Jewish maid who said that a prophet could heal him. When Naaman visited Elisha, he expected the man of God to perform a miracle in might and strength. But Elisha simply said to take a dip in the Jordan River. Naaman became enraged. Here he had done everything he could do to rid himself of leprosy, and he couldn't believe that his promise could come so easily. He had been torn to pieces.

2. The Shunammite Woman's promise of a son (2 Kings 4.8-37): She was a wealthy woman who had no children. She had done everything in her strength to conceive. She could afford the best doctors, and she could support the prophets. By the time Elisha claimed that her promised son would come, she wouldn't believe it. She cried out

for Elisha not to lie to her. She couldn't believe that after all these years, her promised son would come so easily. Her heart had been torn out.

3. The bleeding woman's promise of wholeness (Luke 8.43-48): This woman had spent the last 12 years trying to find a cure for her sickness. She had given up everything to find a cure for her constant bleeding, but nothing and no one could help her. Yet, she saw Jesus and knew that He had the power to restore her. The crowd of people was pressing against Jesus, but in the middle of the chaos, she touched her promise of wholeness by faith, and she was healed. She had developed great faith.

4. Peter's promise of catching fish (Luke 5.1-11): Peter had been fishing all night. He was a skilled fisherman who came from a family of fishermen. He employed all his knowledge and ability all night, but his nets came up empty. Jesus told him to cast his nets one more time. Peter made sure to tell Jesus that he had already done everything in his strength to catch fish, but in obedience, he cast his nets one more time. This time Peter's nets were so full of fish that they ripped, and Jesus said he would now be a fisher of men. Peter was given a purpose.

The reactions of each person give a small glimpse of what God's promises will do to us. God uses them to humble us, renew us, build us and anoint us. God doesn't simply want to bless us; He wants to transform us into a blessing. These promises establish our purpose and teach us to rely on God. But they will tear you to pieces and rip out your heart first.

"Among the other nations, Judah and Israel became symbols of a cursed nation. But no longer! Now I will rescue you and make you both a symbol and a source of blessing. So don't be afraid. Be strong, and get on with rebuilding the Temple!" (Zechariah 8.13 NLT).

Wafers or Loaves

I'm over halfway done doing my 40 days of communion. I specifically asked God to show me more about the Bread of Communion, symbolic of Christ's Body. One day, as I was trying to pour out one of my little communion wafers from the jar, a bunch of them spilled out onto the floor. Since they represent the flesh, I instantly wondered. "Is that how You see us, God? Are we all just a bunch of identical punched-out wafers scattered on the earth?"

I felt God take me to the time of Moses. God wanted a relationship with His people, but in fear they denied such intimacy with God. Instead, they demanded God's rules, claiming that they could keep His Holy Standard in their own strength. That was the day God established the Law, and it was also the beginning of humanity trying to achieve human righteousness without relationship. But we will always fall short of God's glory, and we are desperately in need of a Savior (Romans 3.23).

"Now all the people witnessed the thunderings, the lightning flashes, the sound of the trumpet, and the mountain smoking; and when the people saw it, they trembled and stood afar off. Then they said to Moses, 'You speak with us, and we will hear; but let not God speak with us, lest we die'" (Exodus 20.18-19 NKJV).

When we try to be perfect in our own strength, we'll only gain human perfection, which allows us to appear perfect in the eyes of others and in our own eyes. But this perfect image only shapes us into cookie-cutter imitations of God's best design for us. If we see God as an unloving Master instead of the loving Father, we will be too scared to walk into our destiny by faith.

God created us each uniquely, and we each have a special and specific role to serve in the Body of Christ. When we try to be like someone else, we will all miss our individual calling that has been written in God's scrolls before time began.

"And I saw the dead, great and small, standing before the throne, and books were opened. Another book was opened, which is the book of life. The dead were judged according to what they had done as recorded in the books" (Revelation 20.12 NIV).

The Bible says we are Living Stones, whom God is using to build His Temple on earth. Individually, we house the indwelling of the Holy Spirit, but all Christians, like a family, become a united Temple of God's Presence, and we each fit into a specific niche in the walls of this Temple. Only when we embrace our true design from God will we find our true place in God.

Working with bricks is easy because—just like the communion wafers—they all look the same. However, working with stones takes more time and thought. Each stone is shaped differently, so they are not interchangeable. When we trust God and embrace how He specifically designed us, He will guide us into the destiny He has written out for us. But we must let go of trying to be perfect "bricks" in our own strength and allow the Spirit to shape and guide us according to His will.

We are not all the standard punched-out wafers. We can't judge or covet another person's design and purpose. It may feel safe being just like everyone else, but we won't fit into God's rightful place for us. Instead, we are loaves of bread each with a variety of shapes, textures, aromas and tastes. And God loves how He designed us because He is a creative God, and He wants to offer nourishment to His Creation through our individual ingredients.

"And you are living stones that God is building into his spiritual temple. What's more, you are his holy priests. Through the mediation of Jesus Christ, you offer spiritual sacrifices that please God" (1 Peter 2.5 NLT).

Living Water Garden

"Whoever believes in me, as Scripture has said, rivers of living water will flow from within them" (John 7.38 NIV).

I found myself at the center of a majestic water garden. Tiers of intricate cement stacked themselves one upon another with the angular purpose of allowing the water to charge down like an urban waterfall. I carefully jumped from one giant block to the next, delving deeper into the center of the roaring cascades. I loved the numbing noise. My constant inner analyzing and dialogue halted for the moment as I soaked up the deafening quiet.

Once I got to the core of the water garden, my eyes beheld a 360 view of the force and beauty of the thundering water. Thousands of gallons of glittering liquid circulated down the concrete structure before being sucked into the foundation and pushed back up the stone wall.

I thought of the Living Water. Living Water is the Spirit of God poured out onto the earth through the Redemptive Work of Jesus Christ on the Cross. We live in the New Testament age that the prophets of old longed for and wrote about. We rest in the Great Sabbath because Jesus reconciled us and all the earth back to the Father.

"On that day living water will flow out from Jerusalem, half of it east to the Dead Sea and half of it west to the Mediterranean Sea, in summer and in winter" (Zechariah 14.8 NIV).

The rushing water seemed alive, so I leaned in to touch the glossy facade. I noticed debris speckling the brilliant surface of the water, and indignation rose up in my spirit. It felt unjust that the immaculate image would be blemished by a few fragments.

But then God gave me a metaphor for the Living Water flowing within me. God is perfect, and His Spirit rushes through my spirit and life, pouring out His love, grace and purpose. Since I am not perfect, that Living Water will be marked with my flaws and weakness. What I choose to focus on will dictate my view.

Will I stare only at my mistakes or will I behold the greatness of God in my life? Truth is those mistakes are automatically wiped clean in the eyes of God. Only natural eyes can see them now. If I could glimpse through the Mind of Christ, they would no longer be there. God's Spirit is holy and He can only encompass those who have been purified.

Will I trust my carnal eyes or will I trust the Word of God which declares that I have been made perfect and holy, now and forever? Jesus took all my sins, died with them and left them in the grave when He rose again. The proof that Jesus' Finished Work on the Cross triumphed is that I have the indwelling of God's Spirit. I am beautiful in the sight of God.

"For God's will was for us to be made holy by the sacrifice of the body of Jesus Christ, once for all time" (Hebrews 10.10 NLT).

Grace Umbilical Cord

"For out of His fullness [the superabundance of His grace and truth] we have all received grace upon grace [spiritual blessing upon spiritual blessing, favor upon favor, and gift heaped upon gift]" (John 1.16 AMP).

Grace is something we mention frequently, but I wonder if we truly grasp the profound meaning of this word. Charis is the original Greek word for grace, and the definition of this term includes the following from Blueletter.org:

"That which affords joy, pleasure, delight, sweetness, charm, loveliness: grace of speech…good will, loving-kindness, favour."

We live in a broken world. We can make the best of our situations in this life, but Jesus has provided us through the Cross a power outside of this world that is not affected by our external circumstances. This grace is like an umbilical cord from the Father in heaven to us on earth. It is a lifeline of God's holy goodness that we can believe and receive through faith in the promises found in His Word.

God says He will give us grace upon grace, blessing upon blessing, favor upon favor and gift upon gift—not according to our limited human wants. Rather, this grace is based on a heavenly agenda that sets the stage for God's best in our lives.

Grace is God's fullness poured intravenously through the Vine of Christ into our hearts, minds, bodies and spirits.

"Yes, I am the vine; you are the branches. Those who remain in me, and I in them, will produce much fruit. For apart from me you can do nothing" (John 15.5 NLT).

The goodness of Christ flows when we are rooted in Him. Allow Christ to be God's conduit in your life and receive freely from His grace. Let God know that you need Him each day to live according to His will, and ask Him to show you His spiritual blessings all around you.

"But he gives us more grace. That is why Scripture says: 'God opposes the proud but shows favor to the humble'" (James 4.6 NLT).

Computer Drag

"Therefore, since we are surrounded by such a huge crowd of witnesses to the life of faith, let us strip off every weight that slows us down, especially the sin that so easily trips us up. And let us run with endurance the race God has set before us" (Hebrews 12.1 NLT).

For several months, my computer has been acting up. As I write, several pop-up emergency windows warn me that something is seriously wrong. My emails are not connecting. My phone and computer are unable to communicate. My software runs slowly. And a handful of times I have even had to force shut down my computer.

Not only that, my desktop is a mess. I just finished my 13th book, so I have outlines, documents, edits and cover designs all scattered across my computer's memory. I haven't organized in a while, so I'm constantly searching for what I need.

I've worked under these conditions for some time now. I've been able to get everything done, but I know that I haven't been working at my best. My computer had lots of drag time that was slowing me down. I didn't want to waste time trying to fix everything because I have more important things to do, like write books! But I knew I couldn't ignore the unavoidable for long.

Finally, one morning, I said enough is enough. I sat down at my computer and for the next five hours, I updated, organized, fixed and cleaned my computer. It was frustrating at first because I'm not a computer tech, but little by little I was able to untangle the mess.

Once I was finished, my books were organized, my phone and computer connected, my computer software worked smoothly and I no longer had warning signs popping up, disrupting my work. When I began working on my 14th book, I couldn't believe the ease. I was now working at 100% capacity, and I realized how much my work was slowed down by all the hindrances.

Many scholars believe Paul is the author of Hebrews, and he writes in this book that we should "strip off every weight that slows us down" and "run with the endurance the race God has set before us." Sometimes these "weights" can be huge hindrances that are like boulders on our path, and we have no choice but to call others to help us remove them (doctors, counselors, teachers, etc.). However, most times these "weights" are seemingly small things that can build up over time. We may not even realize that we aren't running at full capacity until it all crashes down around us.

King David wrote in Psalm 139.23: "Search me, O God, and know my heart; test me and know my anxious thoughts."

When we feel the stresses of this world dragging us down, and we know that there are some warning flags popping up in our spirit, it is time to let God search and know us. It does take time, and we may be very busy, but eternity is worth the effort. Life is too short on earth, and we shouldn't live each day dragging weights that slow us down. We can achieve greater peace and purpose if we take time to let God do some maintenance on the inside of us.

God can cut away our burdens and refocus our hearts, minds and spirits. Instead of letting all the burdens build up, it's best to simply seek God every day, allowing Him to search us and pick out those hindrances before they start to affect "the race God has set before us."

"Don't copy the behavior and customs of this world, but let God transform you into a new person by changing the way you think. Then you will learn to know God's will for you, which is good and pleasing and perfect" (Romans 12.2 NLT).

Necklace and Movie

"Ask me and I will tell you remarkable secrets you do not know about things to come" (Jeremiah 33.3 NLT).

Two recent life experiences have taught me a powerful spiritual truth. The first one happened with a necklace I wanted to buy for a friend. And the second with a movie I needed to watch with my husband.

My friend's birthday was coming up and she had just spent several hours editing one of my books, so I wanted to bless her with a special gift. When she was younger and doing missions around the world, God spoke to her in a far-off country with shooting stars. She asked to experience Him in a tangible way, and that night He lit the sky with dozens of shooting stars. So I felt like I needed to give her a shooting star necklace.

When the desire came to me to buy her a necklace, I instantly wanted to start looking for it, but I felt the Holy Spirit tell me to wait for His timing. I put the necklace on the back-burner of my mind, and almost two months later, God said it was time to look. I found the necklace in less than a minute and it was perfect and on sale. That was the necklace God had chosen for my friend.

Another day, I felt like my husband and I needed to watch a movie on the following Tuesday. I kept looking through the movies playing at each theater in town, but nothing looked interesting. I was going to buy tickets for a movie that I didn't want to watch, but God told me just to wait. A few days later, I heard on the Christian radio that a Christian movie event was happening that coming Tuesday—the same day I had in mind. I promptly got our movie tickets to the almost sold-out show. That was the movie God had chosen for us to watch.

God will give us a desire for something, but we must wait on His timing. Many times, we will try in our strength to accomplish this desire, but we will only attain counterfeits. God has something perfect intended for the desire He has placed in us, but it is up to us to trust His timing and not fill the void with our own versions of His best. We can miss out on a major blessing because of our own meddling.

God will allow us to go through small examples like the necklace and the movie until we learn to rely solely on Him. Only then can we be trusted with the bigger desires that He has specifically chosen for us. When God plants a desire in your spirit, wait for Him to show you when to act and resist the urge to force an imitation by your own effort. You can rest in God, knowing that He has the path to your desires with the doors already wide open. We simply need to wait on His timing and respond to His movements.

"Yet I am confident I will see the Lord's goodness
while I am here in the land of the living.
Wait patiently for the Lord.
Be brave and courageous.
Yes, wait patiently for the Lord."
- (Psalm 27.13-14 NLT)

Watered Down Wine

"Your silver has become dross, your choice wine is diluted with water" (Isaiah 1.22 NIV).

Most of the time, water is used as a positive symbol in the Bible—being used as a metaphor for God's Spirit (Isaiah 44.3). However, in the verse above water has a negative connotation because of the context in which it is being used. In the Bible, God relates many spiritual truths to us via metaphors. But we can't always pin a certain symbol in a singular way. For example, Jesus is the Lion of Judah, but the devil is also described as a roaring lion.

Jesus: "Then one of the elders said to me, 'Do not weep! See, the Lion of the tribe of Judah, the Root of David, has triumphed. He is able to open the scroll and its seven seals'" (Revelation 5.5 NIV).

Devil: "Be alert and of sober mind. Your enemy the devil prowls around like a roaring lion looking for someone to devour" (1 Peter 5.8 NIV).

The difference between the capital "L" and the lowercase 'l' is the difference between good and evil and life and death. Therefore, just like anything, we must read the context that encases the symbol in order to make accurate inferences. Isaiah uses the process of purifying silver and the process of watering down wine as metaphors for what is happening to the Children of God. They've stopped allowing God to work in their lives; and instead, they have begun to work in their own efforts to manufacture only what God can accomplish.

Silver is purified in the fires to burn off the dross—the foreign materials in raw silver that need to be removed. God does work in our hearts and minds, cleansing us when we are open to His work in our lives. But we must be receptive to His hand.

Wine can be watered down in order to produce larger amounts; however, the wine will no longer have the quality of its original nature. Humans can water down what God's doing in their lives when they try to reproduce yesterday's revelations, making them counterfeits of today's fresh words.

As we stop relying on God and staying yielded to His authority, two things will begin to occur. First, our unconfessed sin will cause havoc in our natural lives. Supernaturally, we are saved by grace and have been cleansed and purified by the Blood of Jesus Christ. But in the natural our unconfessed sin will litter our hearts and minds like month-old, forgotten trash.

Because of Jesus' Finished Work on the Cross, we will not be judged by our sin, but we will be judged by the vine-rooted works that our vapor-lives have produced (John 15.5, James 4.14 and Matthew 25.23). The dross we allow to build up will greatly hamper our achievement of God's best design and path for our lives that have been written in scrolls before we were born (Revelation 20.12).

Moreover, when we are clouded by unconfessed sin, we won't be able to receive God's fresh revelation every day. We are vessels and are designed to be filled with God's special purposes (2 Timothy 2.21). If we can't attain the outpour of the Holy Spirit, we will begin to water down what little of His revelation we have gained by adding in our own human-centered imaginings and efforts.

In essence, we will dilute God's anointing and power with weak counterfeits that lack power to save and transform lives. We may seem charismatic and sanctified at first, but eventually the wine will run thin, and all that will be left is our own fanciful proclamations and actions.

Yet, as long as we seek God daily and remain in fellowship with Him, we can trust that He will renew our hearts and minds. We will never be perfect, but God makes up for our imperfections with His grace (2 Corinthians 12.9). He cares about us and loves us, and He wants to have a relationship with us now and in heaven. He knows we are all flawed, and He will go out of His way (even dying on a cross) to help us live to our highest potential in Christ (Romans 5.8).

He will never let go of His hand of relationship with us once we accept Jesus as our Lord and Savior, but the hand of fellowship is up to us (John 10.28 and 1 John 1.6). Let us hold tightly to the Lord, trusting that He will purify us and give us a fresh revelation each new day (Ephesians 1.17).

"Instead, let the Spirit renew your thoughts and attitudes. Put on your new nature, created to be like God—truly righteous and holy" (Ephesians 4.23-24 NLT).

Four Rivers

Jesus is the River of Living Water, and He pours His Spirit into the Four Rivers found in the Garden of Eden, bringing life-giving energy to the paradise God created for us. The enemy tried to steal our inheritance; but before time began, God bought us back on the Sabbath with the Tree of Life, Jesus, the payment for our sins (Galatians 3.13-15).

These Four Rivers are not only available to us, but they are rightly ours today through the Redemption of the Cross. We are Children of God. We are co-heirs with Christ. Because of God's great grace extended through the Finished Work of Jesus, our lives on the supernatural level are the wellsprings of Eden—life, joy, peace and oneness with the Father. Our faith taps into the continual supply of these Streams, and we have everything we need to live in perfect unison with God (2 Peter 1.3).

FOUR RIVERS

1. The Pishon River means INCREASE. We are not in lack. God is supplying us daily with His increasing anointing (gifts, talents, resources, relationships, wisdom, strength, power, energy,

healing, wholeness, etc.), and our blessings multiply as we seek Him and connect to His Spirit.

2. The Gihon River means BURSTING FORTH. God is giving us breakthroughs of His favor and grace. He abundantly provides to overflowing as we walk in obedience, so our blessings spill over onto those around us.

3. The Tigris River means RAPID. God's movements are powerful and constant. He is never stagnant, and His Holy current is flowing forcefully in our lives. The enemy cannot stand up to God's unstoppable plan.

4. The Euphrates means FRUITFULNESS. The Living Water of God's Spirit prospers every detail of our lives submitted to Him. We can have His fruit in our hearts, lives, families, relationships, careers and ministries. Though the fruit may tarry for a bit in the natural, they are growing and pressing through the supernatural.

Claim these Four Rivers in your life every day. Imagine them feeding your spirit with all that God wants to provide and do!

"Now a river flowed out of Eden to water the garden. And from there it divided and became four rivers. The name of the first is Pishon. It flows around the whole land of Havilah, where there is gold. The gold of that land is good. Bdellium and onyx stone are there. The name of the second river is Gihon. It flows around the whole land of Cush. The name of the third river is Tigris. It flows east of Assyria. And the fourth river is the Euphrates" (Genesis 2.10-14 NLV).

Suffering Books

I recently bought several books. I found one Christian writer who I enjoyed, which led to another, which led to another, and so on. After a week of Amazon deliveries, I had about a dozen books that I wanted to read. I told my husband as I stared at my stack of books, "Wouldn't it be nice if I could absorb all this information in an instant?" And that's when 1 Peter 4.13 popped into my mind.

"But rejoice inasmuch as you participate in the sufferings of Christ, so that you may be overjoyed when his glory is revealed" (1 Peter 4.13 NIV).

I can't gain the information without turning each page. I can't enjoy the glory (the highest manifestation of God's best) without the suffering.

So many times, we think of the suffering as only the actual Crucifixion, and the thought becomes so overwhelming that we dismiss the possibility of Christ's glory in our lives because the Cross seems unattainable to us. But the Cross is the ultimate demonstration of each choice we make each day—both big and small. The Cross is a lifestyle of "suffering" through difficulty with joy because we see the victory of glory on the other side of it.

- I spend time exercising for the joy of the highest manifestation of health.

- I spend time with my family for the joy of the highest manifestation of relationship.

- I spend time reading my Bible for the joy of the highest manifestation of wisdom.

- I spend time with the Lord for the joy of the highest manifestation of intimacy.

- I spend time serving others for the joy of the highest manifestation of Christlikeness.

The reward outshines the work, and I have joy because I envision the end result.

"Where there is no prophetic vision the people cast off restraint, but blessed is he who keeps the law" (Proverbs 29.18 ESV).

Suffering is a choice we make every day. We will not have the highest without the struggle. It seems like an oxymoron, and it is that glory cannot manifest without the suffering. But this is what Jesus exemplified in His life. He Who is Divine became Servant to all. The King became the Slave (Philippians 2.7). We must not run away from suffering, especially the small choices we make every day. God can use every single second spent in prayer, in a book, in family time, in exercise and in service to establish His highest glory in your life.

"We do this by keeping our eyes on Jesus, the champion who initiates and perfects our faith. Because of the joy awaiting him, he endured the cross, disregarding its shame. Now he is seated in the place of honor beside God's throne" (Hebrews 12.2 NLT).

Baking Promises

"For the revelation awaits an appointed time; it speaks of the end and will not prove false. Though it linger, wait for it; it will certainly come and will not delay" (Habakkuk 2.3 NIV).

In the past few years, I've developed a knack for cooking and baking. I think that now since my three kids have gotten a little older, I have time and energy to be more creative in the kitchen. This morning my daughter and I made our special banana chocolate chip muffins. I can trust that my daughter will be my sous chef anytime the recipe calls for chocolate. The aspect I love most about baking—besides eating—is that there is immediate gratification for my efforts.

I mix the ingredients, pour the batter into a pan, place the pan into the oven and in a few minutes, my creation is complete. Everyone in the family gets to enjoy the fruits of my labor. This is a nice reprieve from a lifestyle of faith that calls for years of waiting on God's promises to come to fruition.

The Bible is full of stories of men and women reaching their God-given promises after years and years of waiting.

- Joseph had to wait in slavery and jail for his promise to be second in command.

- Hannah had to wait in barrenness for her promise of a son, Samuel the prophet.

- David had to wait in the caves for his promise of kingship.

- Paul had to wait for years making tents for his promise of an apostolic ministry.

- The entire nation of Israel had to wait hundreds of years for their promise of a Messiah.

God calls us years before He commissions us. And the time in-between is spent preparing us. There is no other way around the wilderness to our Promise Land. The longer we delay entering into the desert places of our promises, the longer it will take to walk into our victory.

I've grown accustomed to waiting because I trust that God's promises are sure and true. I don't doubt. I don't become discouraged. I am confident that "He who began a good work in you will carry it on to completion until the day of Christ Jesus" (Philippians 1.6 NIV). I wait on God, work towards my promises by faith and enjoy the small things in life that produce immediate results, like banana chocolate chip muffins.

"For no matter how many promises God has made, they are 'Yes' in Christ. And so through him the 'Amen' is spoken by us to the glory of God" (2 Corinthians 1.20 NIV).

I pray that this collection of musings has blessed you. If you enjoyed this book, I would be grateful for a review on Amazon. You can find my other non-fiction and fiction books there or on my blog, www.alisahopewagner.com

- *alisa*

www.ingramcontent.com/pod-product-compliance
Lightning Source LLC
LaVergne TN
LVHW051547070426
835507LV00021B/2453